Making Collector Plates On Your Scroll Saw

by Judy Gale Roberts and Jerry Booher

FOX CHAPEL

Fox Chapel Publishing
Box 7948
Lancaster, PA 17604

Publisher: Alan Giagnocavo
Project Editor: Ayleen Stellhorn

ISBN # 1-56523-050-7

Photography: Jerry Booher, interior
UMI Productions, exterior

Look in the back of this book for information on products used in this book and for other patterns and resources available from the author.

To order your copy of this book,
please send check or money order for cover price plus $2.50 to:

Fox Chapel Book Orders
Box 7948
Lancaster, PA 17604-7948

Try your favorite book supplier first!

Printed in China

Safety First

Before getting started, we want to urge you to develop good safety practices any time you are using any type of woodworking machinery or hand tools, as well as using good common sense when using finishes of any kind. Please make safety glasses and hearing protection standard procedure when using any type of machinery. Be sure to read and follow manufacturers recommendations for safety measures when using power tools and finishes.

Table of Contents

About the Authors

Judy Gale Roberts is an internationally recognized woodworking artist. Her amazing design concepts and woodworking skills have led to her recognition as one of today's foremost woodworking artists.

Judy and her husband Jerry Booher, a master craftsman in his own right, have long expressed their creativity in wood. Together, they have been successful in reviving an ancient Italian art form called Intarsia, the art of inlay. Their credits include an instructional video and a book, *Easy to Make Wood Inlay Projects*. More than one hundred of Judy's original Intarsia designs have been sold to a worldwide audience.

In 1992, Judy and Jerry published their first scroll-saw fretwork pattern book, *Fine Line Design*. Filled with patterns and samples based on Judy's unique style and designs, their first book was an immediate success. The husband-and-wife team now have six scroll-saw fretwork books in their *Fine Line Design* library. Judy and Jerry plan to publish up to twenty volumes over the next few years. This book on using a scroll saw to create collector plates is just one more example of the creativity of this award-winning couple.

Judy and Jerry dedicate this plate book to all woodworkers who are looking for that something special for that someone special in their lives.

Introduction

Using a scroll saw to create your own collector plates from wood is not only a new idea, it's also fun. This fresh look at creative collector plates is just one more way to use scroll saws to unleash the creativity of the individual hobbyist and professional woodworker alike.

There seems to be no end to the design possibilities for scroll-sawed plates. By combining different subject matter in the center of the plate and different sayings and slogans around the outer rim, you can create a multitude of patterns. You can even personalize plates for a special occasion, or use them as gifts for friends and loved ones. Each plate will no doubt be treasured for many years to come.

The decorating possibilities of scroll-sawed plates are also boundless. By using colored fabric, cardboard, or paper behind the fretwork cutouts, each plate can be custom decorated to fit any decor. You can also apply paint, glitter, sequins, and ribbon. More detail can be added through woodburning, engraving, or relief carving. With all this versatility, scroll-sawed collector plates will surely become one of the most popular woodworking ideas to come along in years.

The plate designs included in this book are the creation of professional artist Judy Gale Roberts and craftsman Jerry Booher. Each plate design has been carefully thought out to ensure that each is unique, as well as "shop tested." You'll find detailed instructions that will lead you step-by-step through the making of a scroll-sawed plate, plus a variety of patterns that can be customized for many special occasions. A Buyers' Guide in the back of the book provides a list of suppliers for products used in this book.

1
Plate Preparation

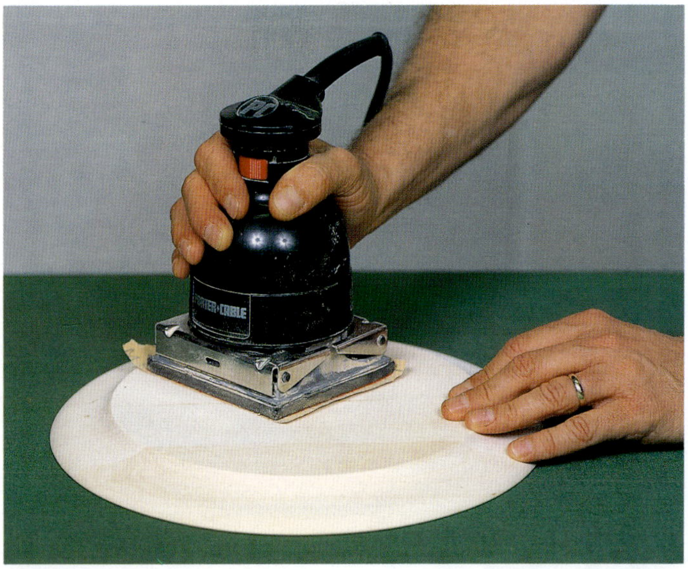

Illus. 1-01 *Turn the plate face down and sand the back with a palm sander or by hand using 120-grit sandpaper.*

The designs included in this book will fit wooden plates with a 12" outside diameter. You can make your own plate on a wood lathe; you'll find a pattern in the pattern section on page 48. Or you can purchase plates specifically made for this purpose at your local woodworking store or through a mail-order catalog. Whether you spin your own plate or use a pre-made plate, there is a certain amount of preparation that needs be done before you begin cutting a design.

First, sand your plate by hand with a piece of 120-grit sandpaper or a palm sander. Lay the plate face down **(Illus. 1-01)**, and sand the back first. Once the back is sanded smooth, turn the plate over and sand the front. Start by sanding the wide rim, and then move to the drop center **(Illus. 1-02)**. Once the front and the back side are sanded, carefully sand the outside edge by hand to remove any scratches or fuzz.

Next, remove all the dust particles from the front and the back of the plate by using a soft brush to gently dust the plate. Finish dusting the plate with several blows of compressed air. If you feel an extra dusting step is needed, gently wipe the plate with your bare hands to remove any dust particles that may have been left behind.

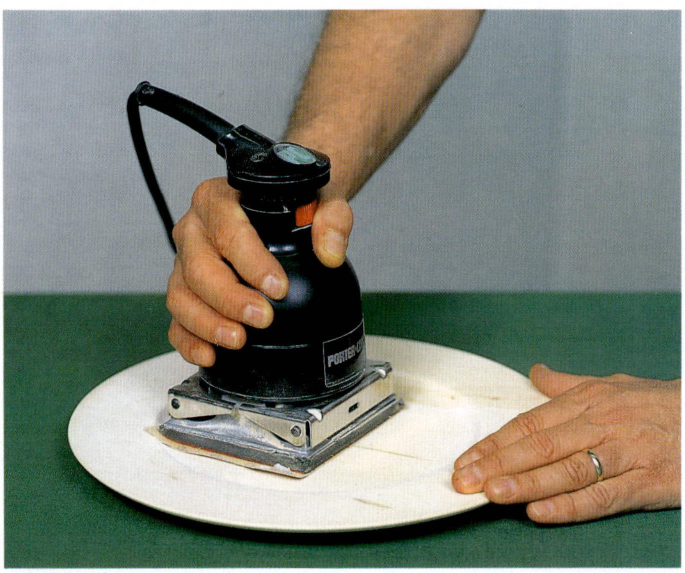

Illus. 1-02 *Turn the plate over and sand the outer rim first. Then sand the center of the plate.*

When you are satisfied that your plate is sanded smooth and free of dust particles, it is time to apply a finish to the plate. You can use any method you like. Spraying the plate with lacquer or acrylic or a clear enamel are several popular choices. Whichever method you prefer, we recommend that you apply a finish before you begin to cut. You can also choose to leave the plate natural, that is, not apply any finish.

We commonly use a wiping gel finish. This method has

proven to be the best method for us to achieve a near-perfect finish every time. The tools needed to apply a gel finish are minimal—a 1-inch disposable foam brush and a roll of paper towels.

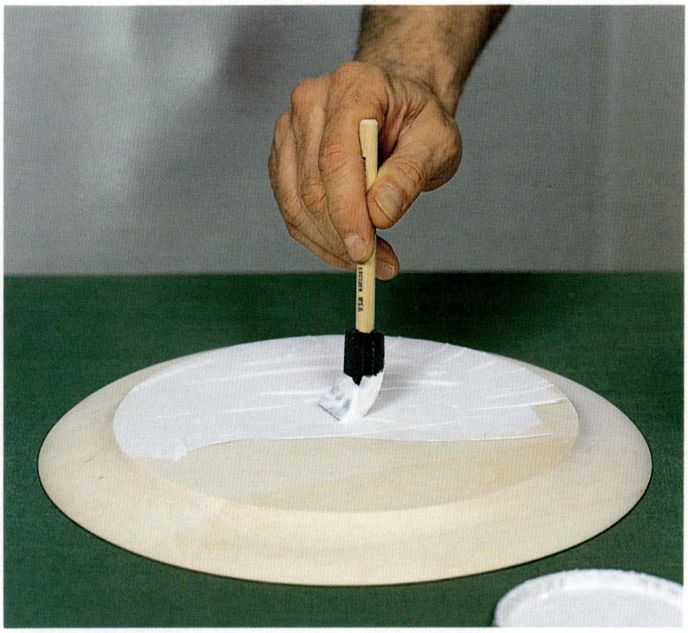

Illus. 1-03 *Cover the entire back of the plate and the edge of the rim with a generous coat of white stain wiping gel.*

We have found that when using a clear finish gel, the white wood of commercially available plates has a tendency to yellow or darken. To avoid this discoloration, we prefer to use a white stain gel instead of a clear gel for the first coat, followed by another coat of the white stain gel or a coat of clear gel. We normally use one coat of white stain gel and one coat of clear. Two or three coats will do the job. In the can, the white stain will look very white, almost like a white paint. But when it is wiped off, only a small amount of white remains in the grain of the wood. Remember that the more coats of white stain gel you use, the whiter the plate's surface will become.

Apply the first coat of gel to the back of the plate **(Illus. 1-03)**. Cover the entire back and the very edge of the rim. Don't be stingy with the gel—we always apply a good heavy coat—and don't worry about brush marks or excessive build up. After only a minute or so, wipe off all of the gel with paper towels until no gel is left on the plate. We use several paper towels for this part of the job—the first one gets off the bulk of the gel; two or three clean ones finish the job; and one final paper towel is used to wipe off the plate in the direction of the grain. It may seem counterproductive to wipe off all the gel we just put on, but the finish will turn out just great. The gel will soak into the wood in just a minute or two's time. Promise.

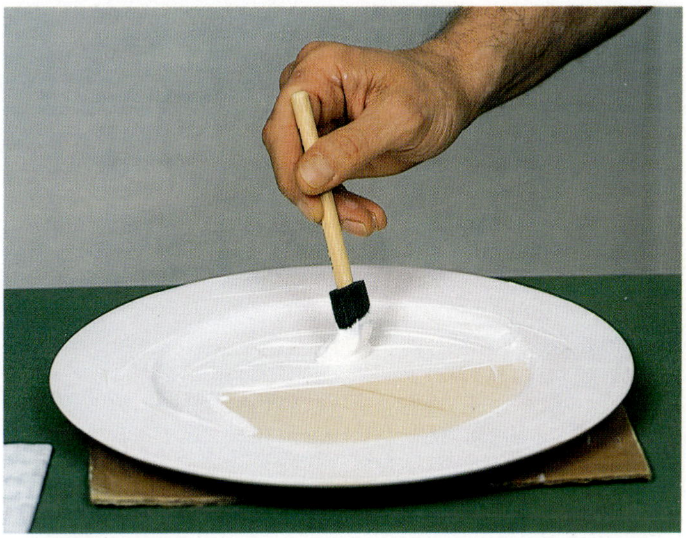

Illus. 1-04 *Apply a generous coat of gel to the front of the plate.*

Now turn the plate over and apply a coat of gel to the front of the plate **(Illus. 1-04)**. Again, give the plate a

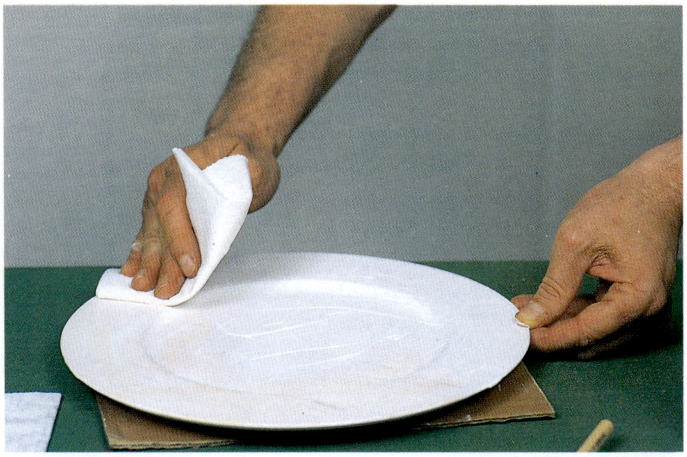

Illus. 1-05 *A minute or two after applying the gel, wipe the excess gel from the plate.*

heavy coat of gel, making sure to cover the plate completely. Allow this coat to sit for only a minute or two, and then wipe off the excess gel. Finally, using a clean paper towel, wipe the plate in the direction of the grain, as you did on the back **(Illus.1-05)**.

Rest the plate on an angle and let it dry four to six hours until the finish is completely dry **(Illus. 1-06)**. While the plate is drying, store your used brush in a plastic bag until you need it for the next coat. The brush will last for several days this way.

After the first coat has dried thoroughly, apply a second coat to the front and to the back. Use either another coat of white stain gel or a coat of clear gel. If you are switching to a clear gel for this coat, be sure to use a different 1-inch foam rubber brush. Use the gel in the same manner as the first coat, applying generous amounts of gel to the back of the plate first and then moving to the front. Allow the second coat to dry four to six hours. Generally, two coats of gel is plenty, but you may want to apply a third coat. Experiment to find out what works best for you.

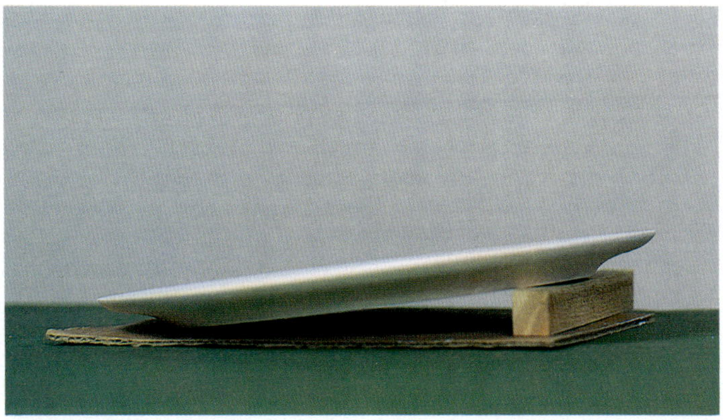

Illus. 1-06 *Place a small block under one end of the plate and let the plate dry in this position for four to six hours.*

To clean up your hands after you are done applying the finish, use a waterless hand cleaner, like mechanics use. This type of cleaner is much better for your hands than harsh chemicals.

2

Applying the Pattern

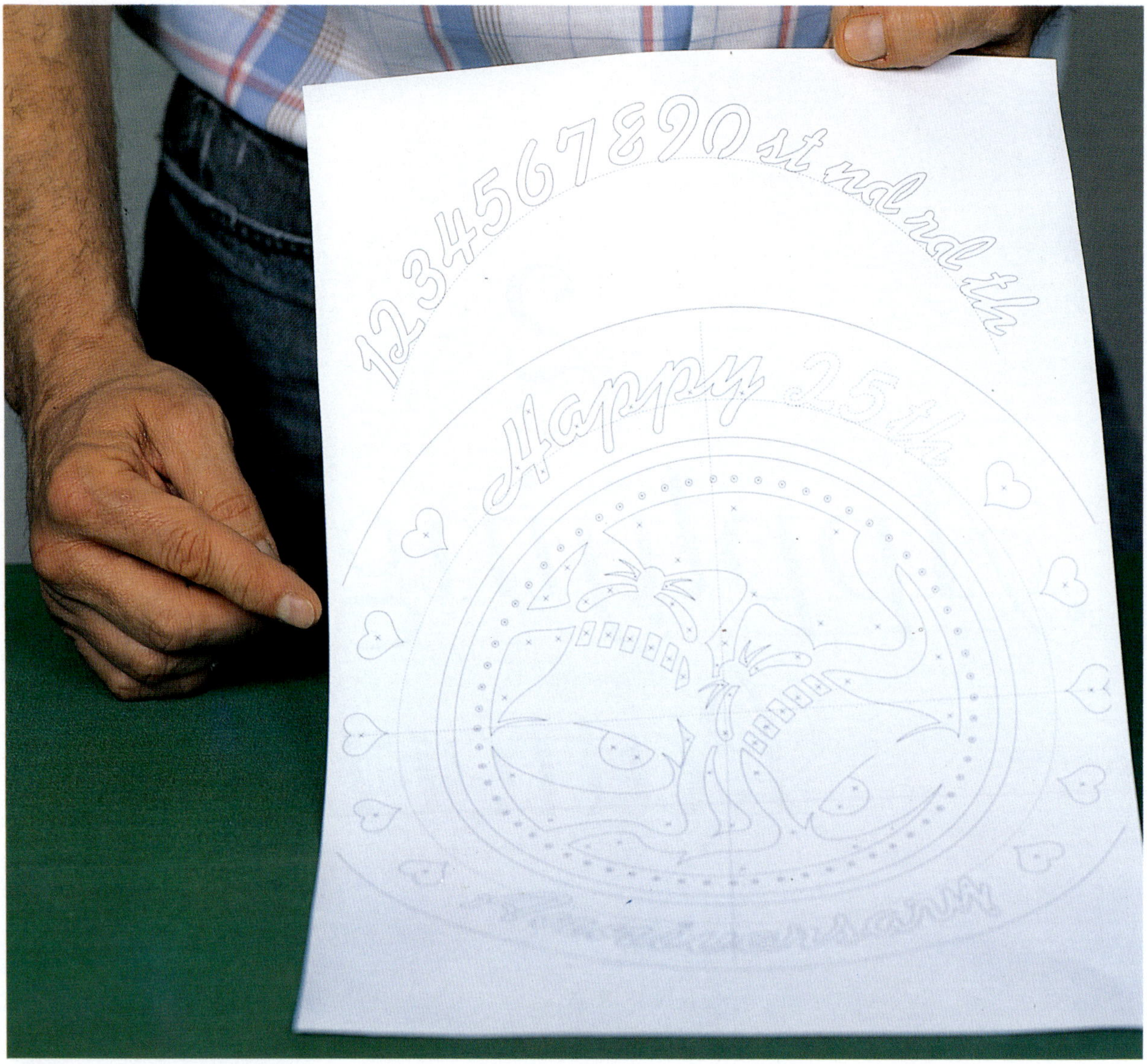

Illus. 2-01 *The outer edges of the pattern will not print when you enlarge the pattern to 200% on an 11" x 17" piece of paper. Just position the pattern so the missing parts are on the left and right sides of the plate.*

Applying the pattern to the plate is a simple procedure. However, there are a few things you need to be aware of before you start. If you are planning to use the patterns in this book, you will have to enlarge them 200% on a photo copier. It is easiest to use a photo copier that can handle 11" x 17" sheets of paper. You can also enlarge the pattern in sections, using the dashed lines as guides, if a bigger copier is not available.

If you enlarge the pattern on an 11" x 17" piece of paper, you will notice that part of the outside ring does not appear on the enlarged pattern. This is because we are enlarging the pattern to 12 inches in diameter, which is one inch larger than the paper width of 11 inches. This is not a problem. Just position the pattern so that the missing parts are on the left and right sides of the plate **(Illus. 2-01)**.

Using a pair of scissors, cut around the outer ring as close to the black line as possible **(Illus. 2-02)**. You will notice that there are two inner rings. The ring closest to the outer edge of the plate marks the edge of the pattern for the rim. The inside rim marks the edge of the pattern for the center of the plate. Cut the larger of the two inner rings first to separate the pattern for the rim from the pattern for the center **(Illus. 2-03)**. Next, cut the smaller ring to remove the extra sliver of paper **(Illus 2-04)**. Discard the thin band of paper you just cut out. We will not be using it. The center of the pattern will now fit into the inner part of the plate.

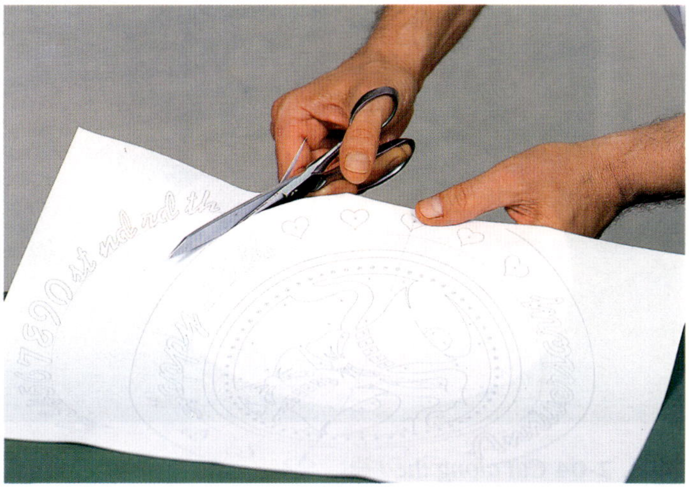

Illus. 2-02 *Cut out the pattern, following as closely as you can to the outermost black ring.*

Place the wooden plate on a flat surface and turn it until the grain runs horizontally (sideways). A grain that runs diagonally will make the design seem off-balance to your eye.

Use a spray adhesive or rubber cement to apply the inner pattern to the plate. Be sure that the adhesive you use is not a permanent adhesive. Read the label carefully to ensure that you are using a temporary adhesive. If you have any doubts about the adhesive you are about to use, test it on a scrap piece of paper and a scrap piece of wood. You want the paper to stick well to the wood, but not so well that it will not "release" when you are ready to remove it. It is always best to read the directions first and follow the manufacturer's recommendations before proceeding. If your spray adhesive does not release easily, but instead starts to pull the paper apart leaving paper traces on your plate, try using a hair dryer to apply heat to the pattern. The heat will make it easier to pull up the pattern. This has saved us many times in the past.

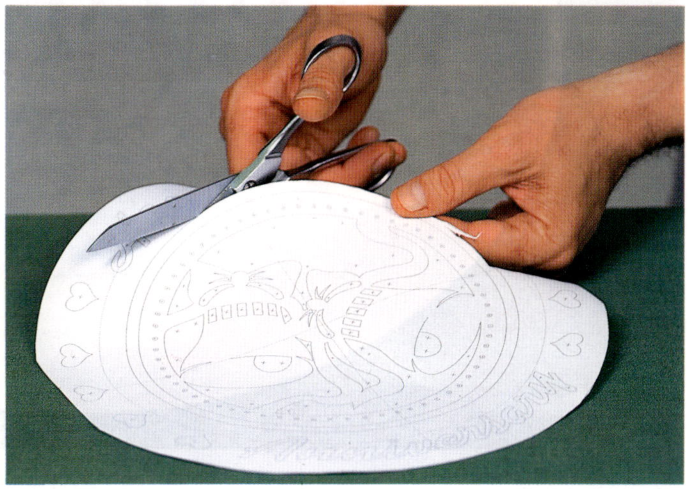

Illus. 2-03 *Cut around the outermost inner ring.*

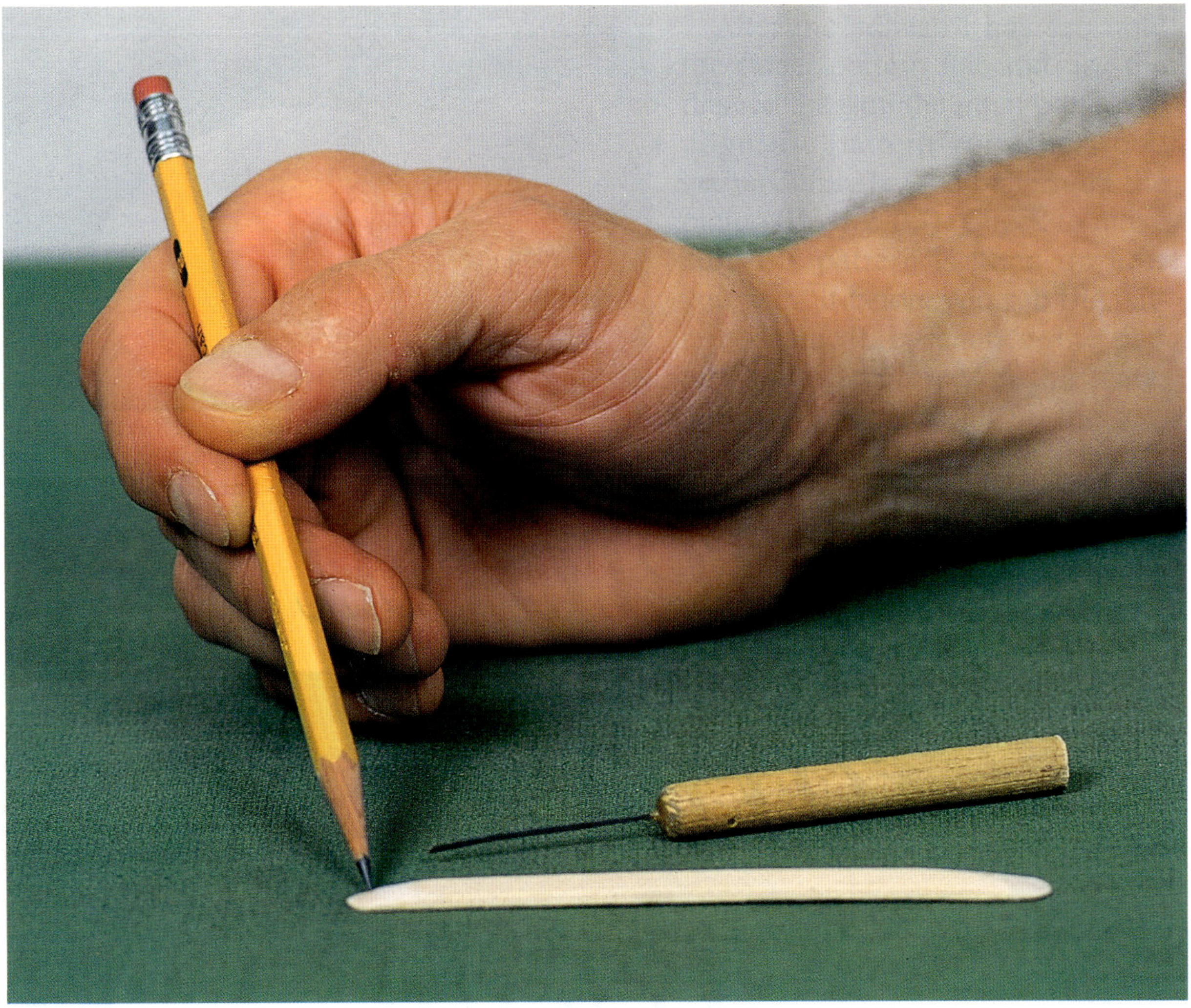

Illus. 3-01 *Two simple homemade tools, a pointed popsicle stick and a broken saw blade, can make scroll sawing easier.*

Before we continue with sawing the plate, we would like to show you a couple simple, homemade tools that have helped us a great deal with our scroll sawing **(Illus. 3-01)**.

The first tool is a wooden popsicle stick. I have sanded an angle on each end of the stick following the rounded end. This stick is a priceless tool. Use it to hold the pattern down if your pattern starts to lift off the wood as you cut **(Illus. 3-02)**. (Oh, by the way, it is best to eat the popsicle first!) In case you don't like popsicles and can't swipe one from the kids, you can find them in craft supplies shops under the name craft sticks.

The second tool is a broken scroll-saw blade, which I have glued in the end of a dowel. Just use a dowel about 3/8" or 1/2" in diameter and about three inches long. Drill a clearance hole in the end of the dowel large enough for the blade to slide in freely. The hole in the tool pictured here is about

1/2" deep or so. We use a broken #4 or #6 blade. The blade should be long enough to bottom out in the drilled hole and extend out the end 1 1/2" to 2". Glue the blade into the hole. We use woodworkers glue, but you may want to use a different kind. After the glue has dried, sand the end of the blade so that any sharp burrs or corners are removed and smooth to the touch.

Use this tool to remove a stubborn drop-off piece from its cut-out area **(Illus. 3-03)**. Just lift the plate off the table a little and poke the drop-off piece out the bottom. We have found it best to remove the drop-out piece before unthreading the blade. If you try to unthread the blade with the drop-out piece still in the hole, the piece can act as a wedge against the blade, making it almost impossible to unthread the blade without bending it or twisting it to the point that it can't be used for the next cut.

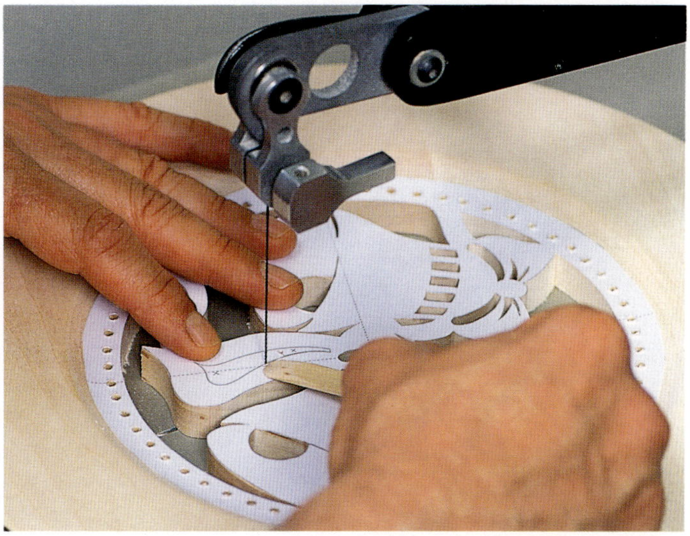

Illus. 3-02 *Use a sharpened popsicle stick to hold down a pattern that lifts up.*

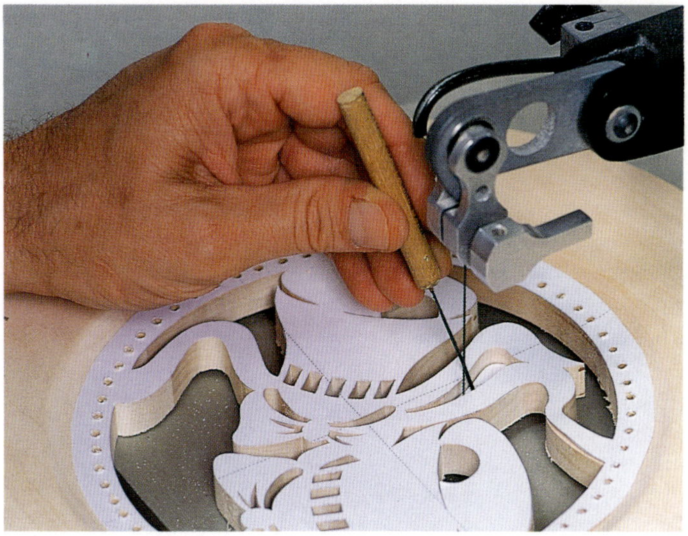

Illus. 3-03 *A broken saw blade glued into the end of a dowel will help you to remove a stuck cutout.*

4

Sawing the Center

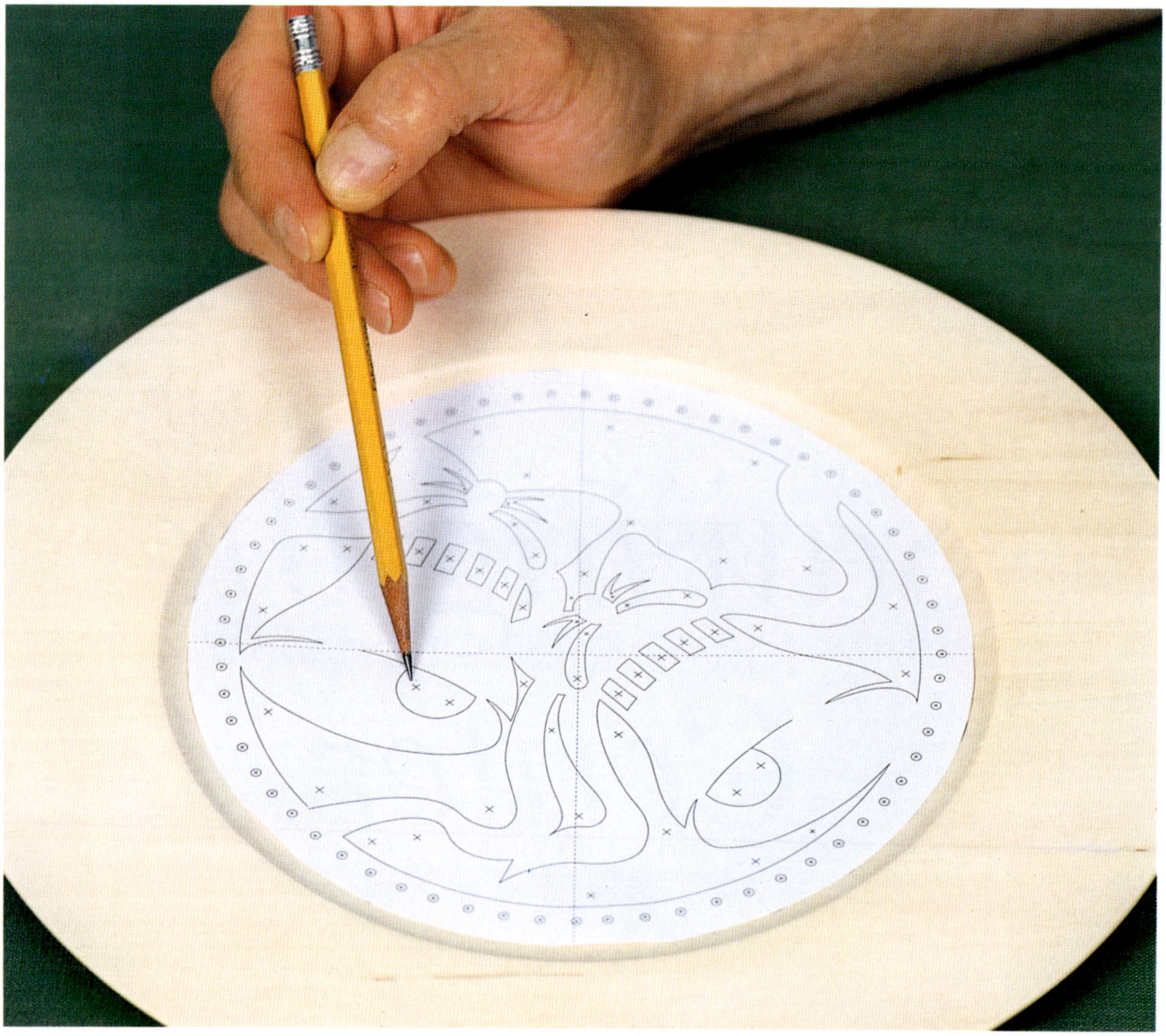

Illus. 4-01 *The X's on the pattern indicate pieces of the plate to be cut out.*

Now that you have couple of helpful tools close at hand, the real fun begins. Take a few moments to look at the pattern. You will notice that there are many areas marked with X's. These X's indicate areas to be cut out **(Illus. 4-01)**.

To remove wood from these areas, you must first drill a small hole in each area through which the scroll-saw blade will be threaded. I have made it standard practice to drill more than one hole in each of the larger areas **(Illus. 4-02)**. These extra holes will give you a relief area to head for in case your blade gets dull and needs to be changed. You can also use these extra holes as a new starting point in the event that you break a blade. If you thread the blade through the original start hole after changing blades, you will almost always have to retrace the old cut until you reach the point where you had to stop when your blade broke. By retracing a cut, you run the risk of accidentally cutting into the plate as you rapidly run your new blade along the old cut. If you have to retrace a cut, don't panic. Just be careful not to gouge the good part. Careful planning really pays off when doing fretwork.

After drilling the start holes in the areas to be cut out, you can now begin cutting the plate design. Use a #2 or #4 plain-end blade. As a general rule of thumb, we like to start with the simple, small areas first. This gives us time to get in the swing of things. We then gradually move on to the larger, more difficult areas. We save the most fragile areas for last. This way there is less chance of breaking the pieces off while handling the plate.

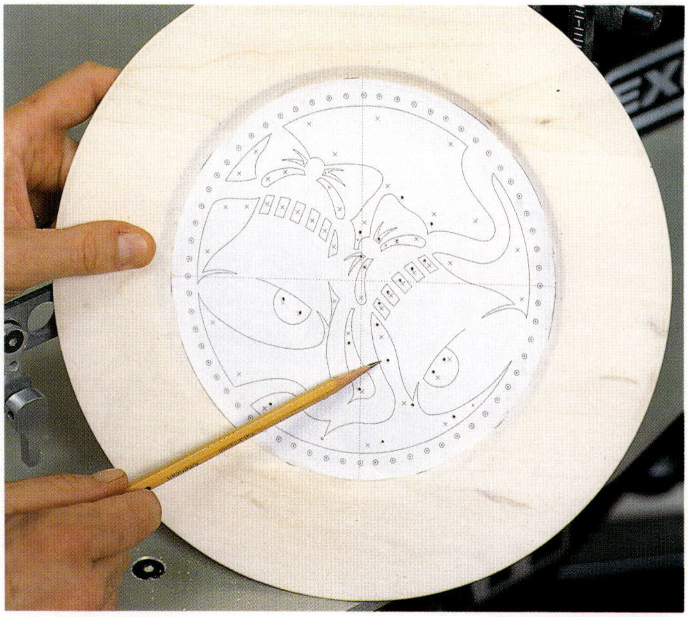

Illus. 4-02 *Drill a small hole in each area to be cut out. These holes will provide starting places for your blade. Drill more than one hole in larger areas.*

Round circles on the pattern can be made with a drill that closely matches the size of the circle. This method is easier than trying to drill a start hole and then sawing. But beware, oval areas will have to be drilled and then cut with the scroll saw, instead of just drilled. These areas are meant to be ovals, and if they are drilled, the round shape will change the overall effect of the design.

Once all the areas have been cut out and you are satisfied with your cuts, turn the plate over and sand away the burrs on the back of the plate with 120- to 180-grit sandpaper **(Illus. 4-03)**. These burrs are caused by the downward cutting stroke of the blade. If the burrs are allowed to remain, the plate will not sit flat on the scroll-saw table and will have a tendency to vibrate or "bang" as you cut the outer rim. When all the burrs have been sanded away, turn the plate over once again with the inner pattern still in place **(4-04)**. You are now ready to saw the rim.

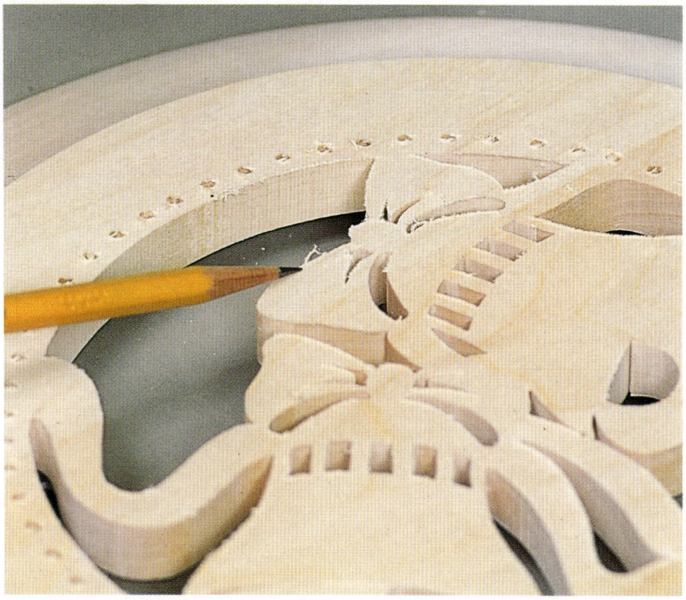

Illus. 4-03 *Leaving the pattern attached, turn the plate over and sand away any burrs left by the downstroke of the scroll-saw blade.*

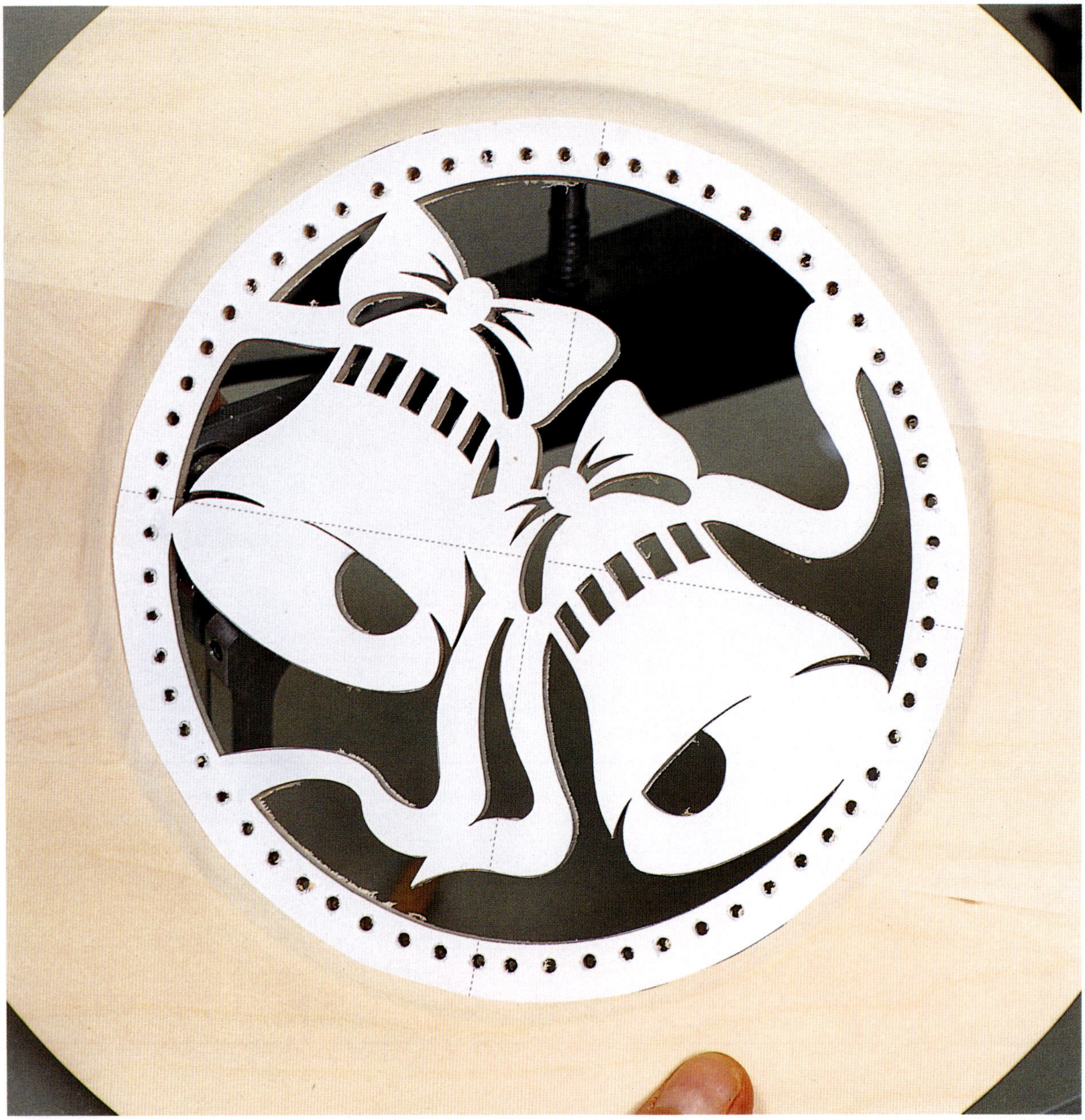

Illus. 4-04 *Leave the pattern attached to the plate even after the center of the plate has been completely cut out.*

5
Sawing the Outer Rim

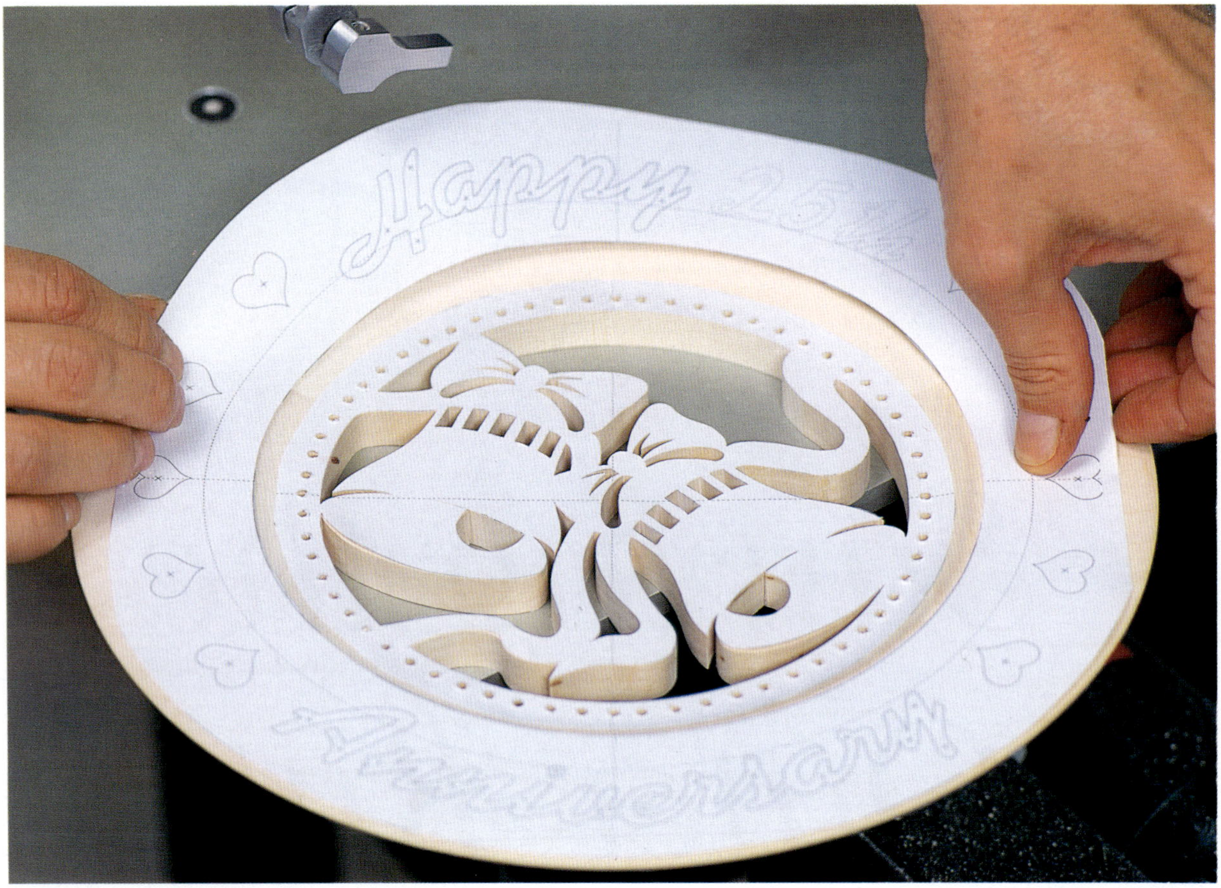

Illus. 5-01 *Rotate the pattern until the dashed lines on the inner pattern and those on the outer pattern are aligned.*

Lining up the pattern on the outer rim of the plate takes some patience. Be sure not to rush. It is especially important when sawing text that the words be balanced and square with the subject matter.

First, turn the plate so that the subject matter is facing you. Using a pencil, extend the vertical and horizontal dashed lines onto the plate. Coat the back of the outer rim pattern with the adhesive. Once the adhesive has set, carefully line up the dashed lines you drew on the plate and the dashed lines on the outer rim pattern. Lay the pattern lightly on the plate. Before you press the pattern into place, look again to make sure that the dashed lines are lined up correctly and that the pattern is centered on the rim. If you are not satisfied with the alignment, lift the pattern and move it to another position **(Illus. 5-01).** When you are satisfied with the alignment, press the paper pattern firmly into place and rub it with your fingertips to ensure a good bond.

Sawing the outer rim of the plate is a little more tricky than sawing the inner design. Because the outer rim of the plate tapers to a thin edge, you will be cutting thick material toward the center of the plate and thinner material toward the outside **(Illus. 5-02)**. The pressure that you need to place on the blade will be constantly changing as you move from thick to thin or thin to thick. The speed of the blade will also vary, becoming slower for thick wood and faster for thin wood. Make a mental note of this thin-to-thick or thick-to-thin condition and adjust your cutting speed accordingly.

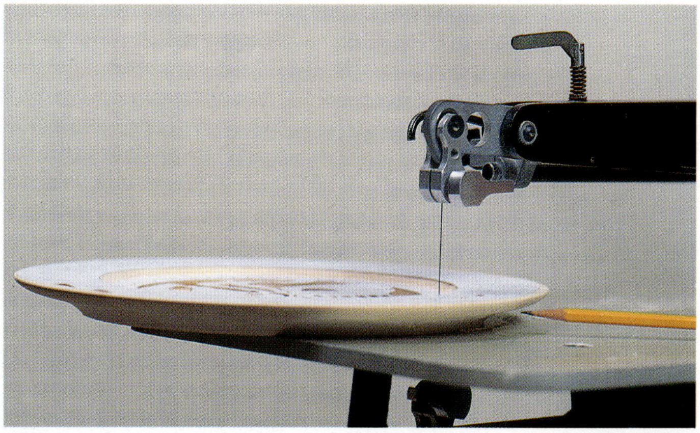

Illus. 5-02 *The tapering of the outer rim may cause the plate to tip as you saw.*

The tapering of the rim will also cause the plate to tip a little. To keep the plate from tipping, place your fingers in the center of the plate and apply light pressure as you saw the rim. Use the fingers on your other hand to hold the plate close to where the cutting is being done **(Illus. 5-03)**.

Begin sawing the outer rim as you began sawing the inner section. First, drill the start holes. If the text or design on the rim calls for a long, detailed cutout, like script text, drill multiple holes as we did on the larger areas of the center design **(Illus 5-04)**.

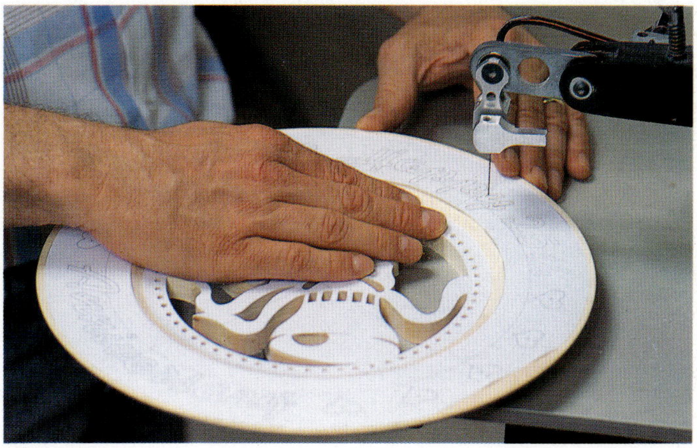

Illus. 5-03 *To keep the plate from tipping, place one hand in the center of the plate and the other on the outer rim.*

I have found it best to cut the outermost part of the text or design first **(Illus. 5-05)**. If you cut the inner part of the text or design first, the outer part will become a little fragile or flimsy, making it more prone to breakage, as well as making it a little more difficult to cut.

After all your cuts have been made, turn the plate over and sand away any burrs that appear on the back of the rim. Use 120- to 180-grit sandpaper.

Once the rim of the plate is cut and sanded, it is time to take a breather. You may want to eat a popsicle (and save the stick) as you inspect all the cutouts to make sure that they are completely cut out and that you are satisfied with your cuts. If you need to trim or touch up any cutouts do it now before removing the pattern.

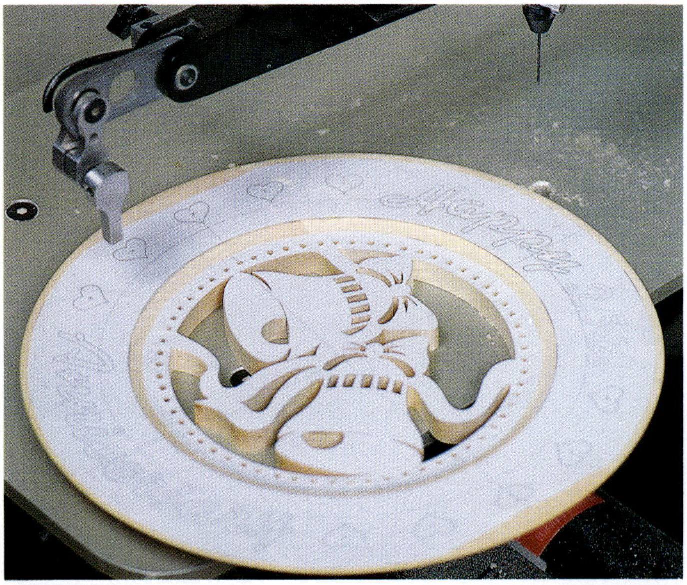

Illus. 5-04 *Drill start holes in each of the sections to be cut out. Drill several holes in larger sections.*

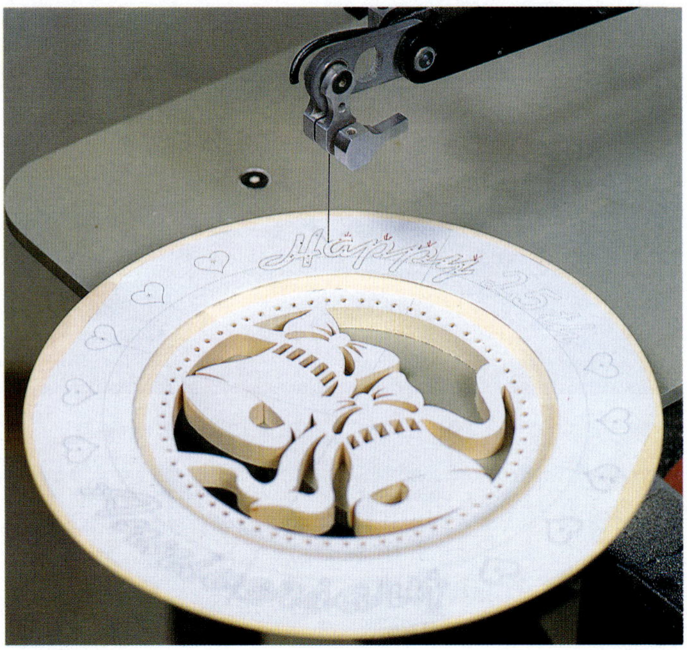

Illus 5-05 *Cut the outermost part of the design first.*

Your very last step is to remove the patterns from the plate. Remember, if the pattern starts to shred as you take it off, use a hair dryer to apply some heat. The heat will lessen the staying power of the adhesive and save you a lot of frustration.

6
Decorating Scroll-Sawed Plates

Engraving

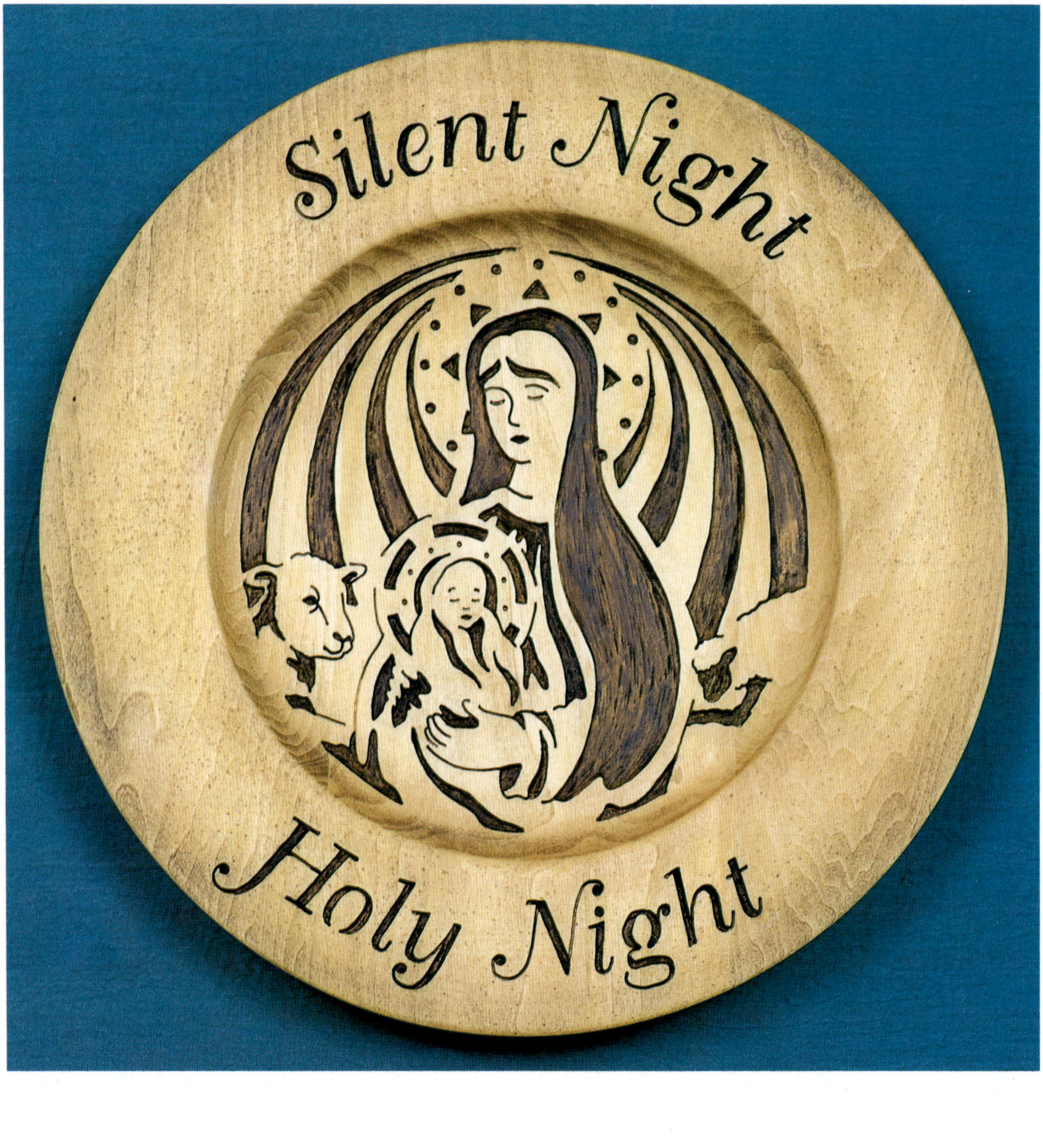

This fantastic engraved plate was made using a hand-held high-speed engraver. As you can see, the design was not cut on a scroll saw, but engraved in the wood. The plate was first finished, and then the design was sketched into the wood. A wood stain, applied after the engraving was finished, adds color to the engraved ares. This model was furnished to us by the Paragrave Corporation, of Orem, Utah.

Wood Burning

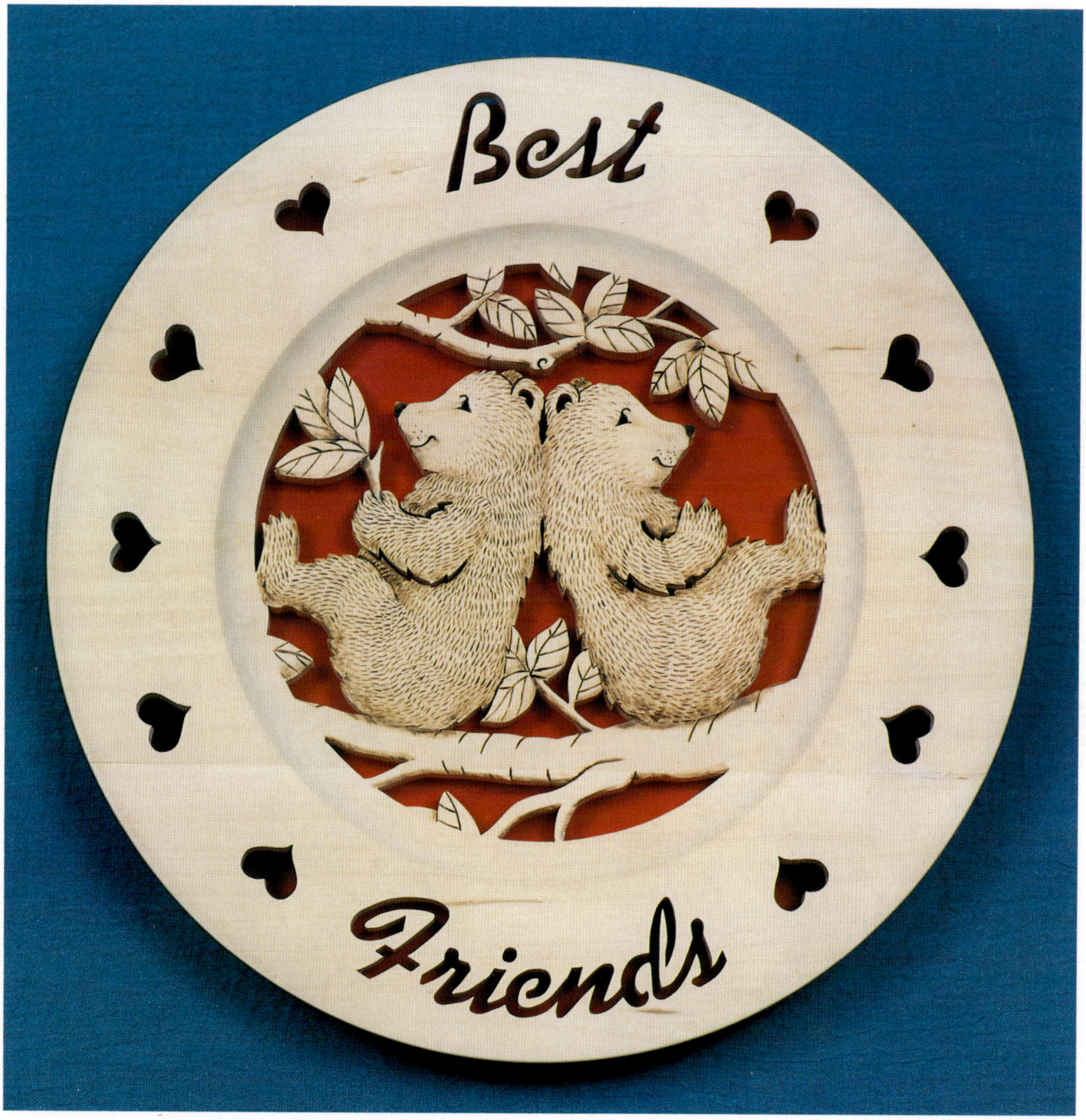

A woodburning tool uses high heat and a metal tip to burn fine lines on wood. Use a woodburner to add detail to a scroll-sawed plate. Different woodburning tips included with the tool will give you different cuts. You can also change the temperature settings to achieve different lines. As you can see from the photo, the scroll-sawed plate really comes to life with the addition of some woodburning.

Clock Plate

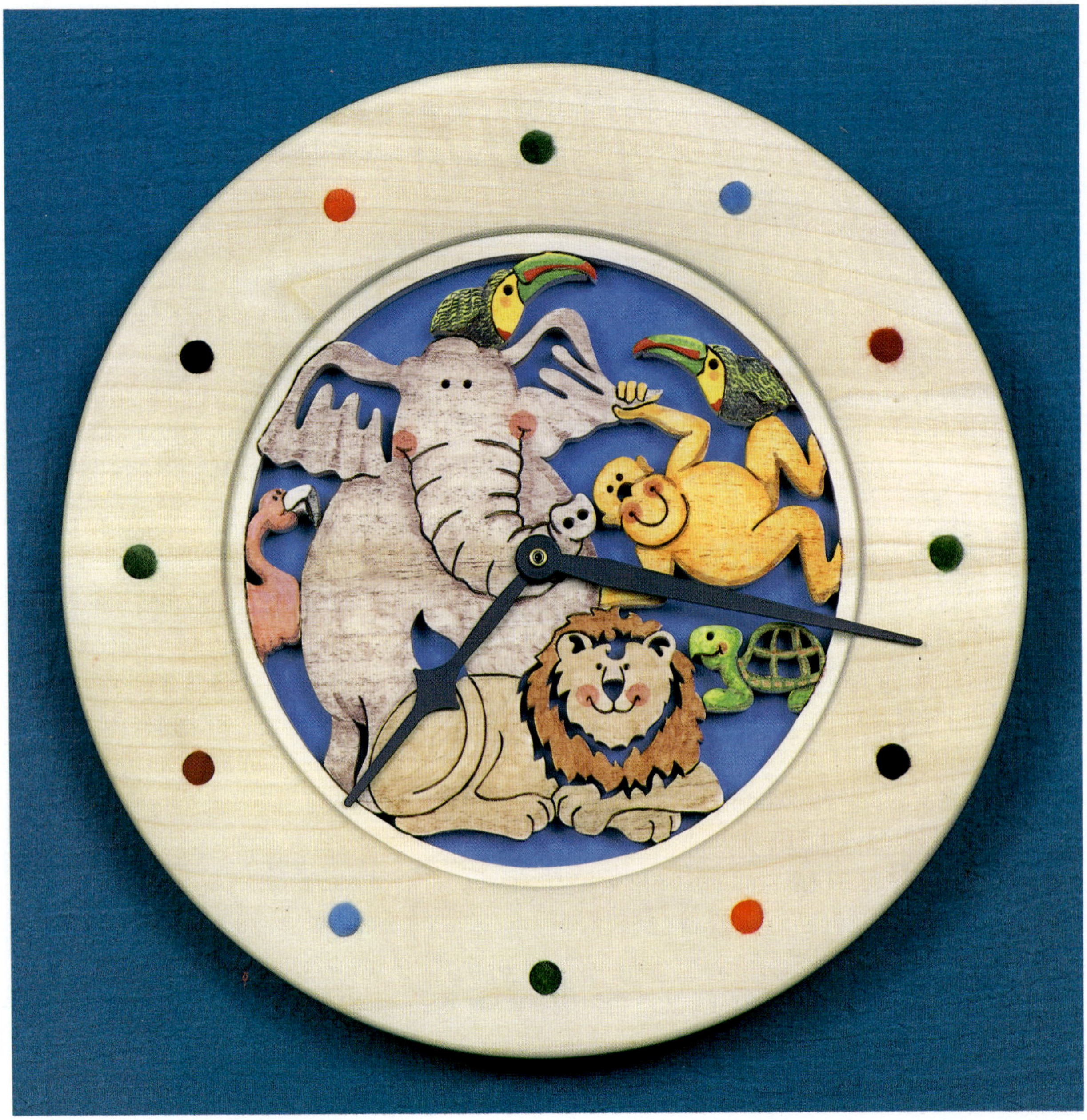

The color that was added to this plate was done with permanent ink markers. Magic markers are a quick and easy way to color wood. We also added a clock movement. The number locations were drilled and filled with pom-poms, which are available at craft supplies stores.

Tole Painting

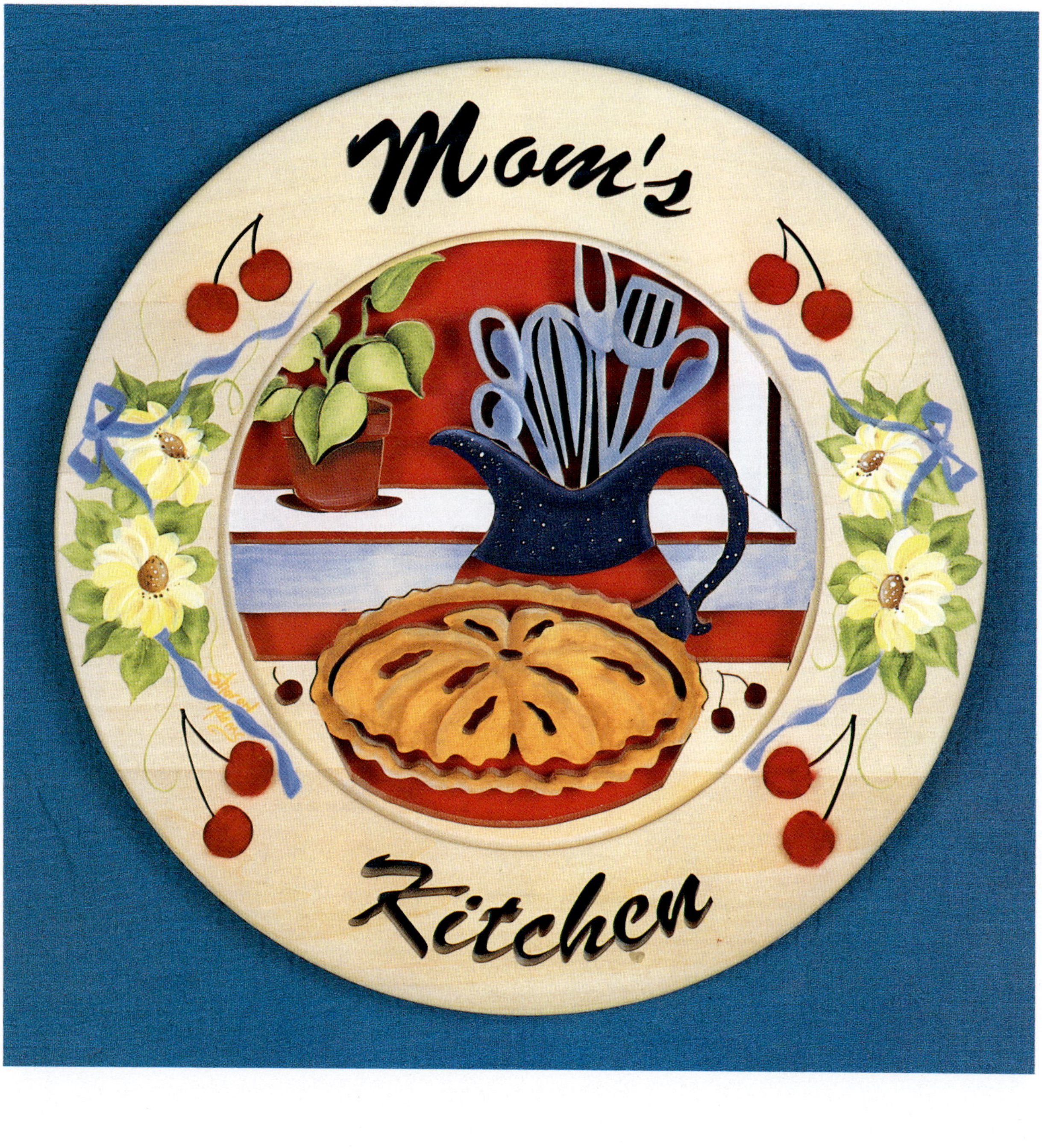

Tole painting is another way to dress up the scroll-sawed plate. This lovely painted plate was furnished to us by Sharon Adams of Lufkin Texas.

Plate Kits

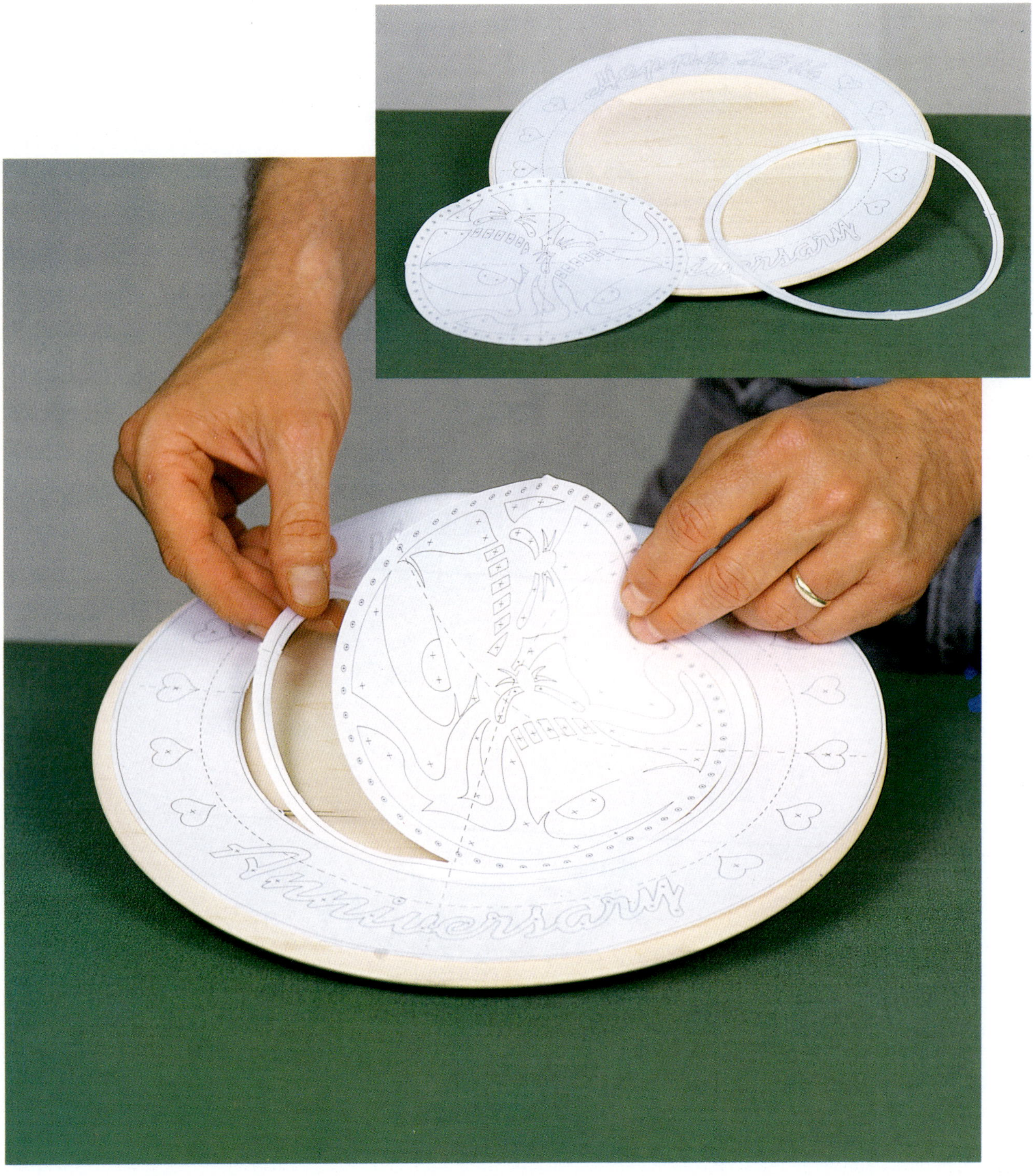

Each pattern featured in this book is also available in a full-size, unfinished version. These full-size patterns come with a pre-made plate that is ready to mount and saw. The patterns come with the outer rim already cut to size. The two inner rings are perforated, making them easy to separate without the use of scissors.

7

Scroll-Sawed Plate Patterns

Best Friends

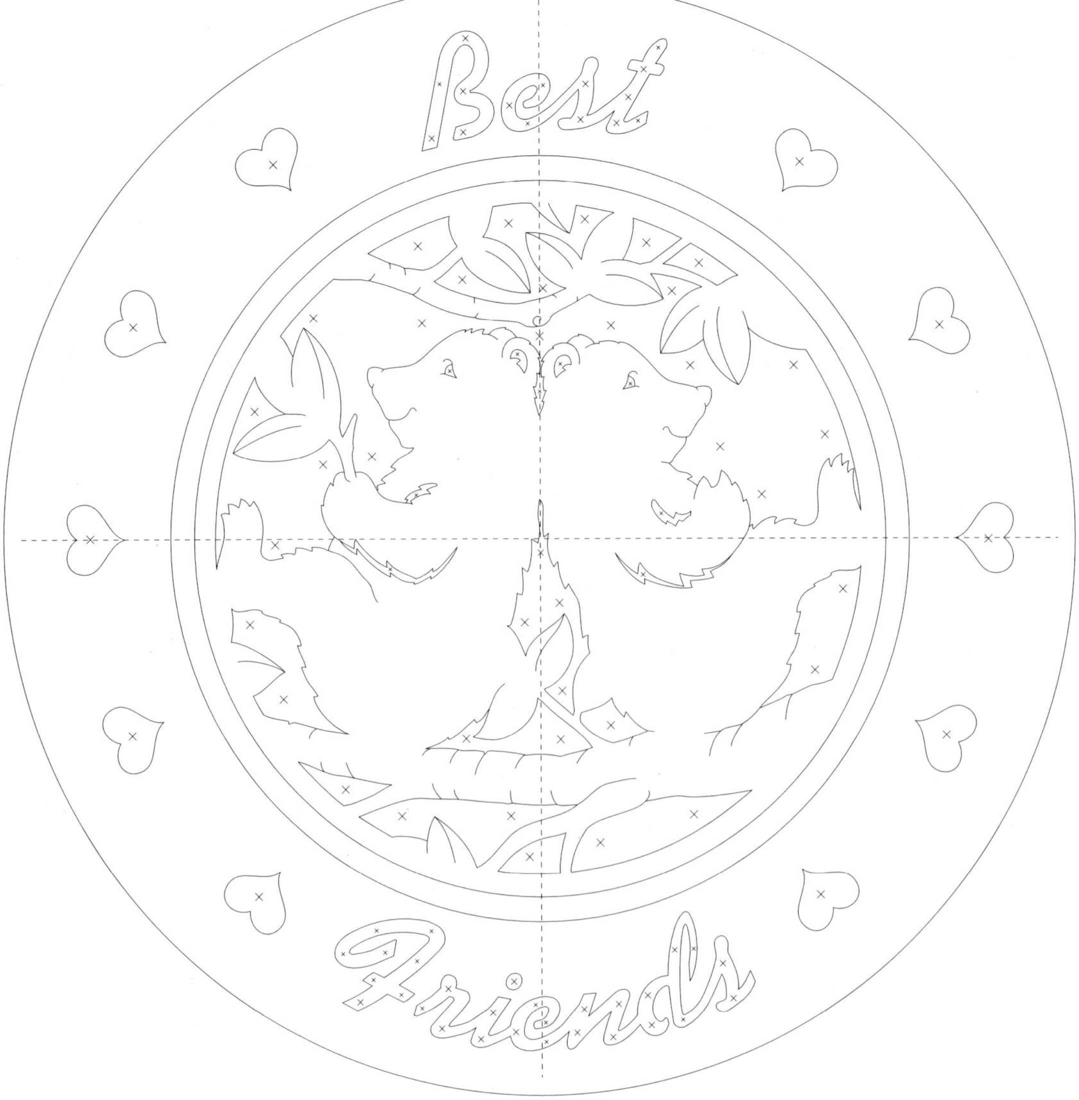

To decorate Best Friends, *use a circle cutter to cut a blue piece of poster board 8" in diameter for the background color. Use either hot glue, epoxy, contact cement, or white glue to permanently attach the poster board to the back of the plate. To accentuate the line work, follow the cut lines with a woodburner. Another idea for this plate includes using 1/2" pom-poms to add color to the hearts. Stuff three pom-poms in each heart. Craft stores generally have a wide variety of colors and sizes available.*

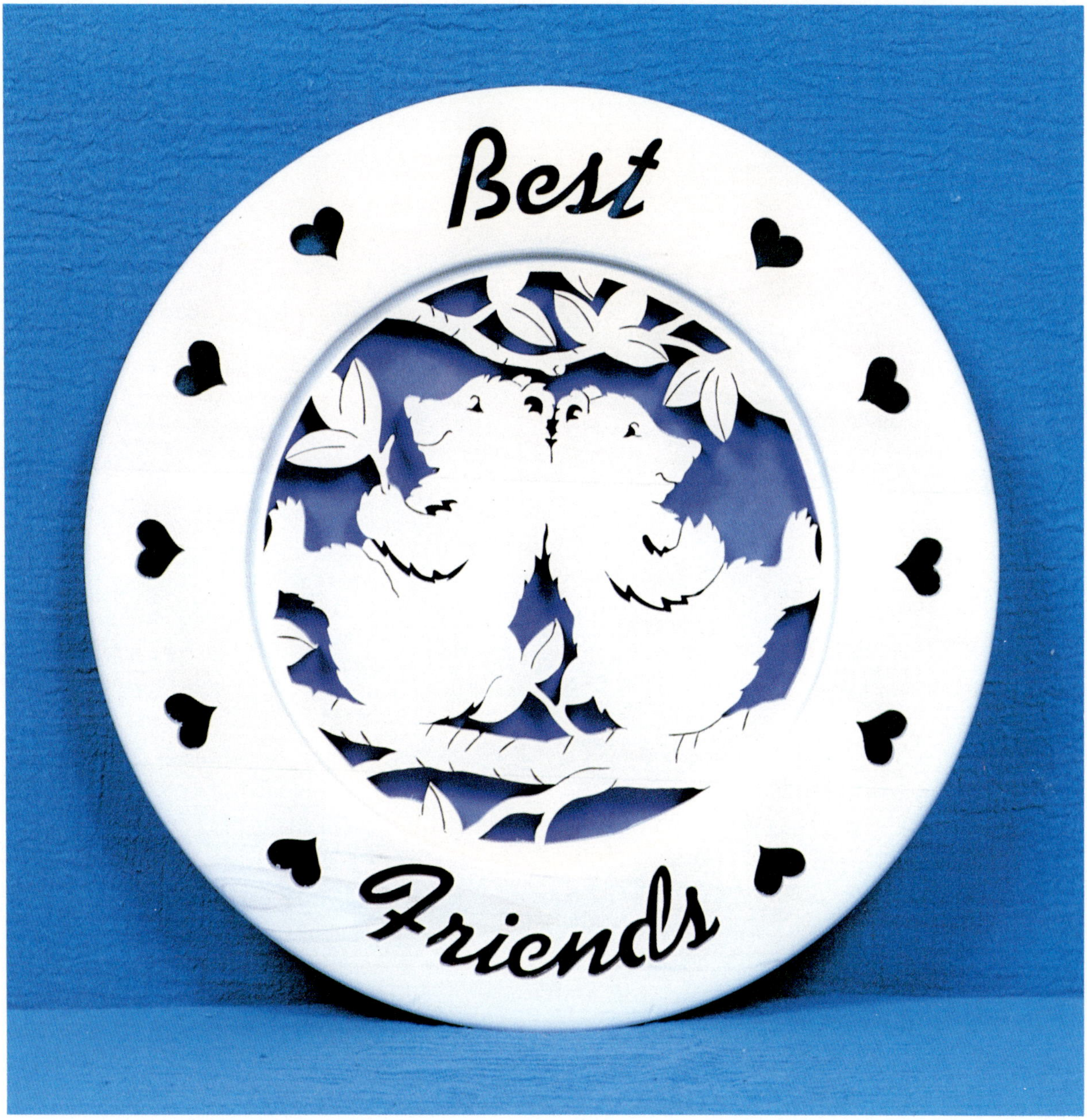
Best
Friends

Expect A Miracle

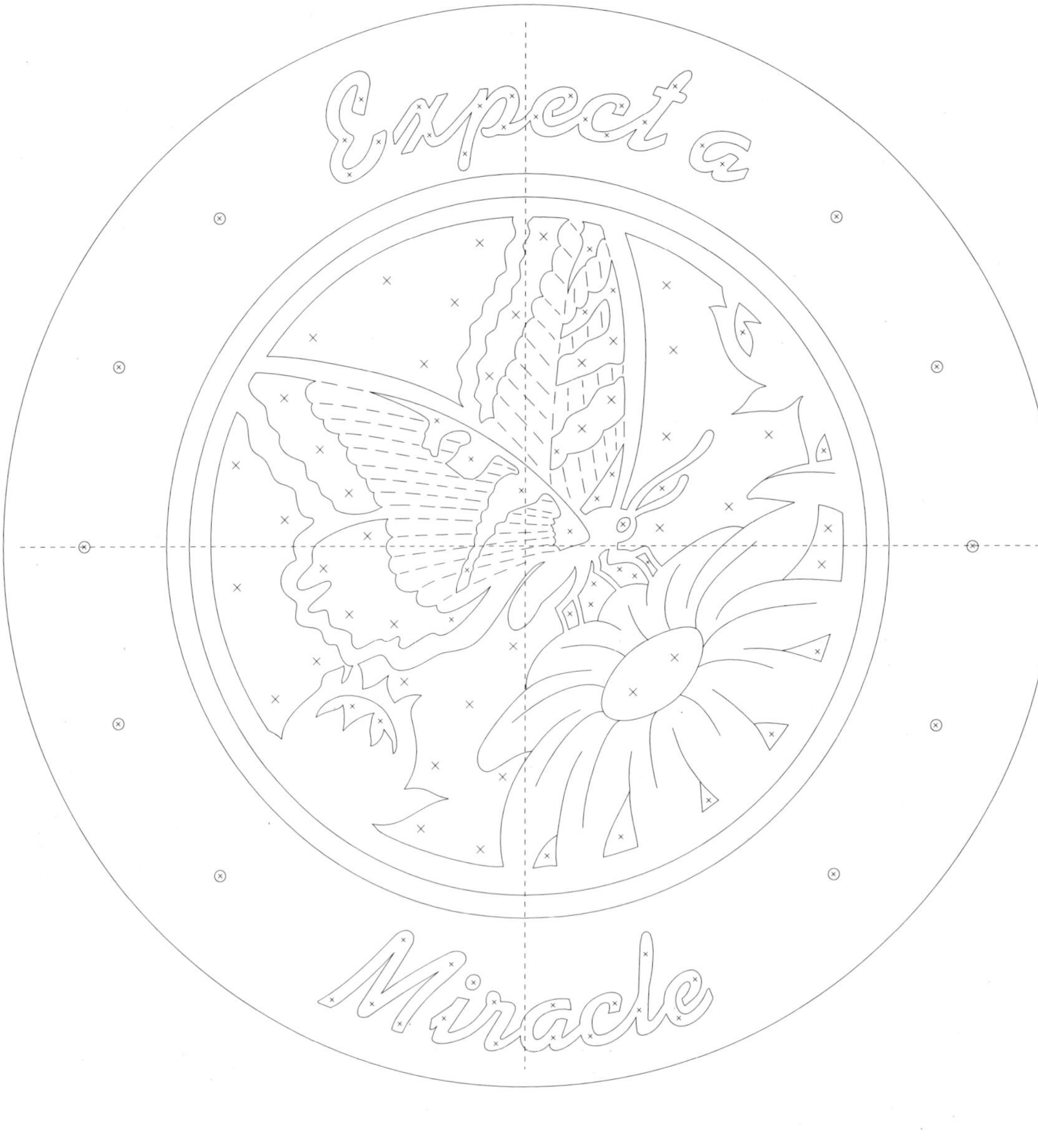

To decorate Expect A Miracle, *use small silk flowers in the drilled areas around the rim. Cut the flower stem to about 1/4". Put hot glue in the drilled hole, then quickly put the flower stem in the glue. Cut the felt or fabric in an 8"-diameter circle and use hot glue, contact cement, white glue, or epoxy to permanently attach the backing to the plate. Use a woodburner to add detail to the butterfly's wings and to accentuate the line work created by the scroll saw. You can also add beads, pom-poms, or silk butterflies instead of flowers around the rim of the plate. Try eliminating the text completely and continuing the decorations evenly around the rim of the plate.*

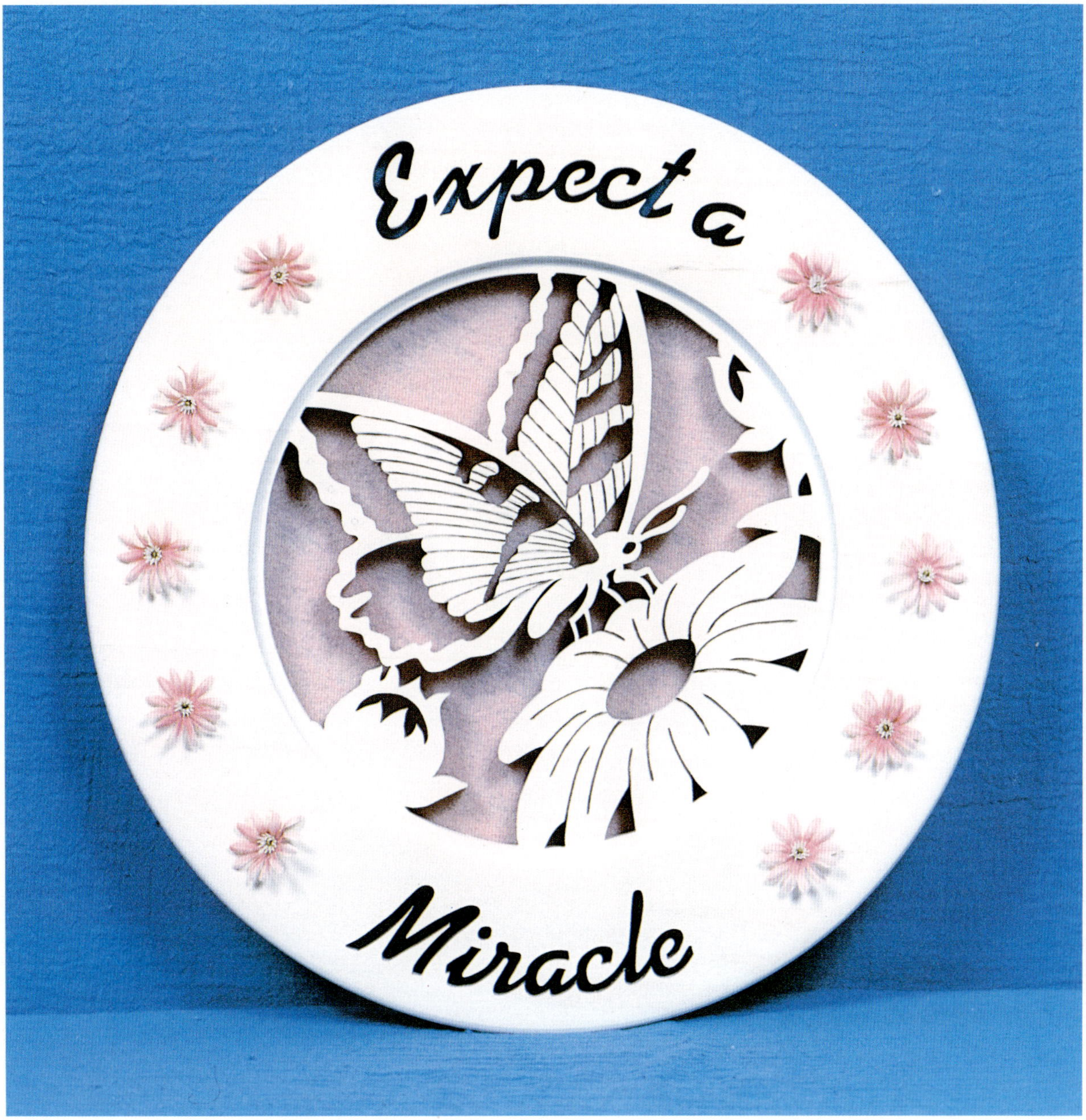
Expect a
Miracle

You Are My Sunshine

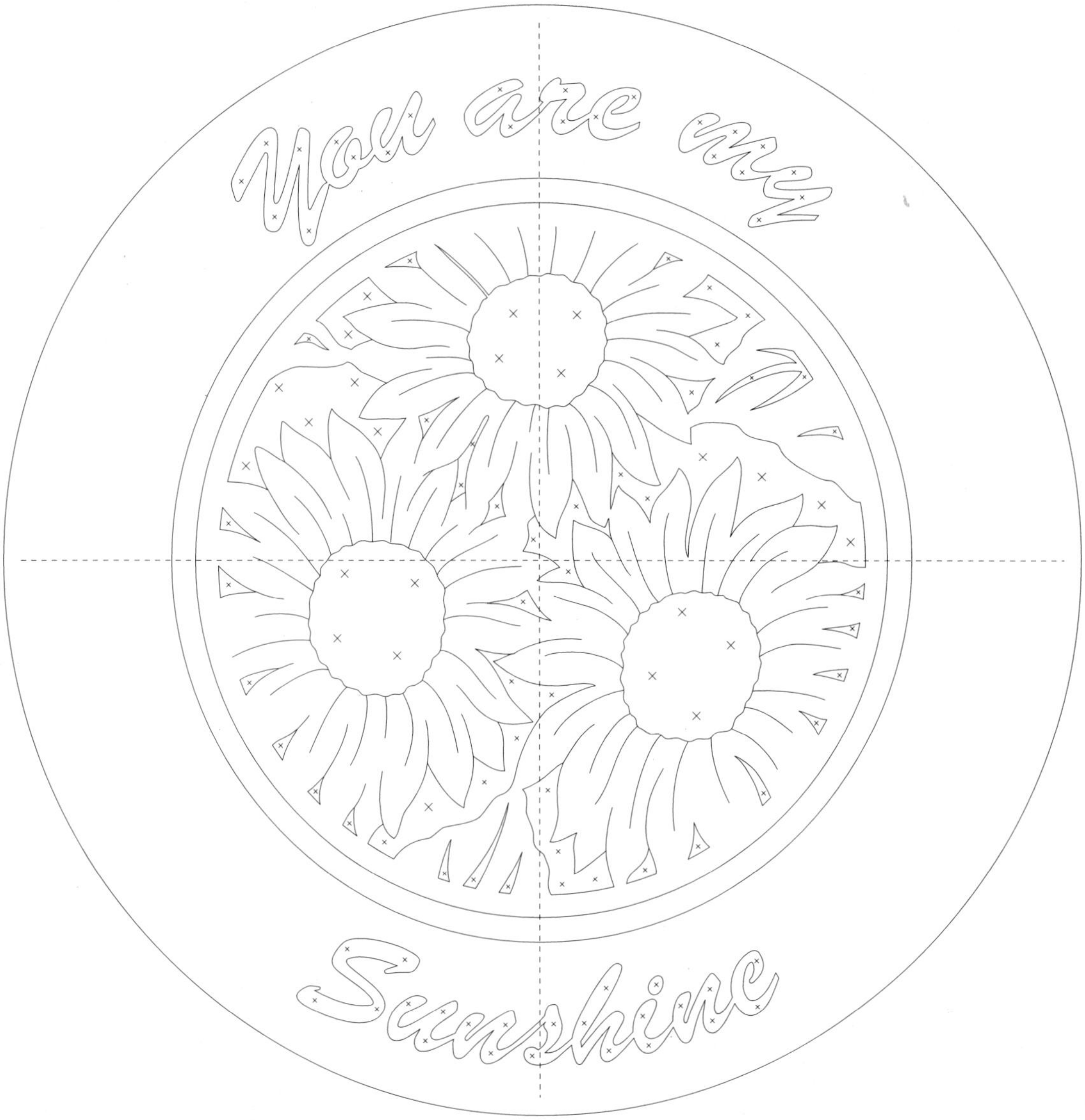

To decorate You Are My Sunshine, *cut an 8"-diameter circle from a piece of gold fabric and use hot glue, epoxy, or white glue to permanently attach the fabric to the back of the plate. Use only the center section and the two inner rows of petals from the silk sunflowers. Put hot glue in each cutout, and then quickly add the flower section. You may also want to drill some holes around the rim and glue different color beads, small flowers, small bows, or pom-poms in the drilled sections.*

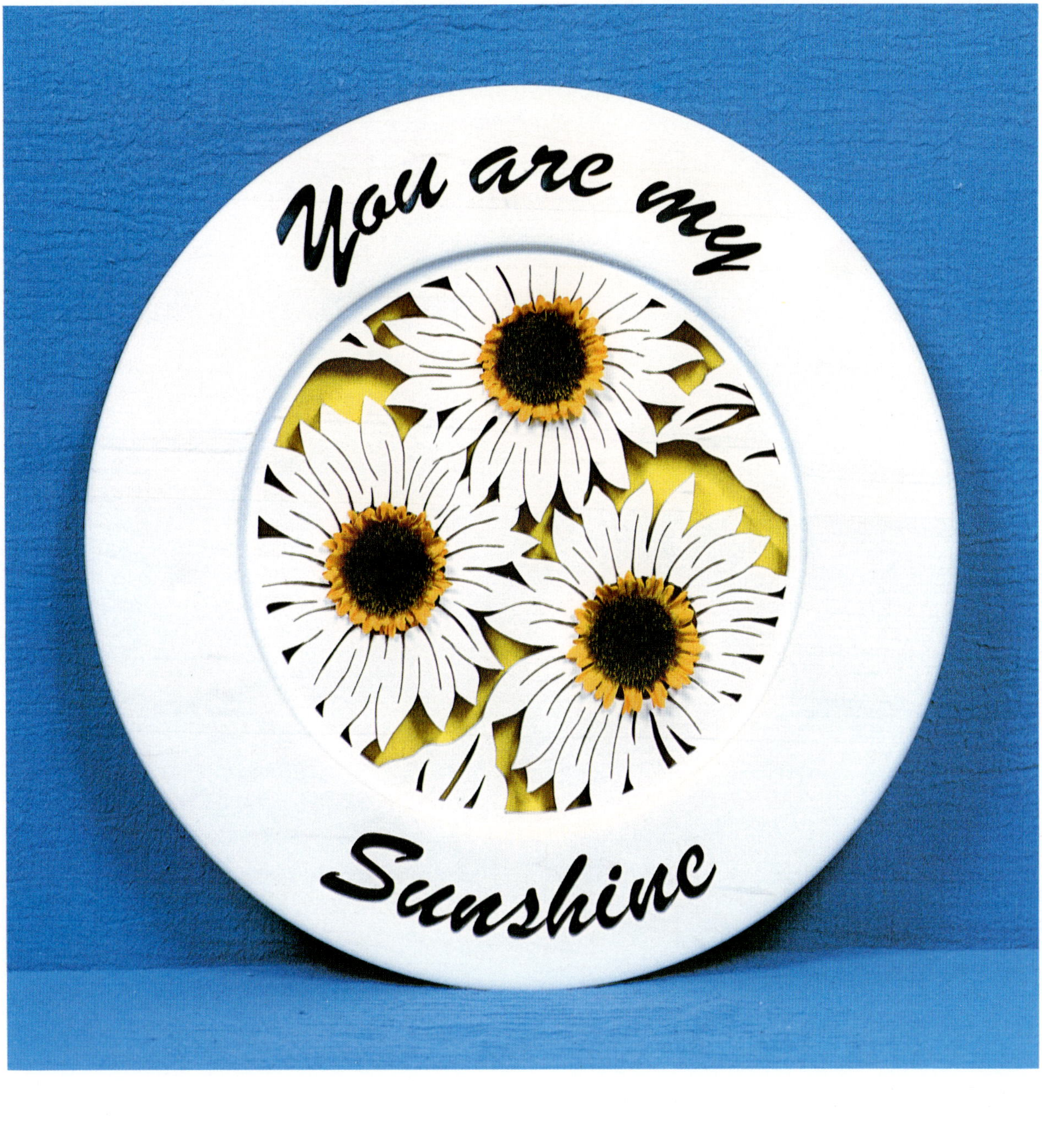
You are my
Sunshine

Silent Night

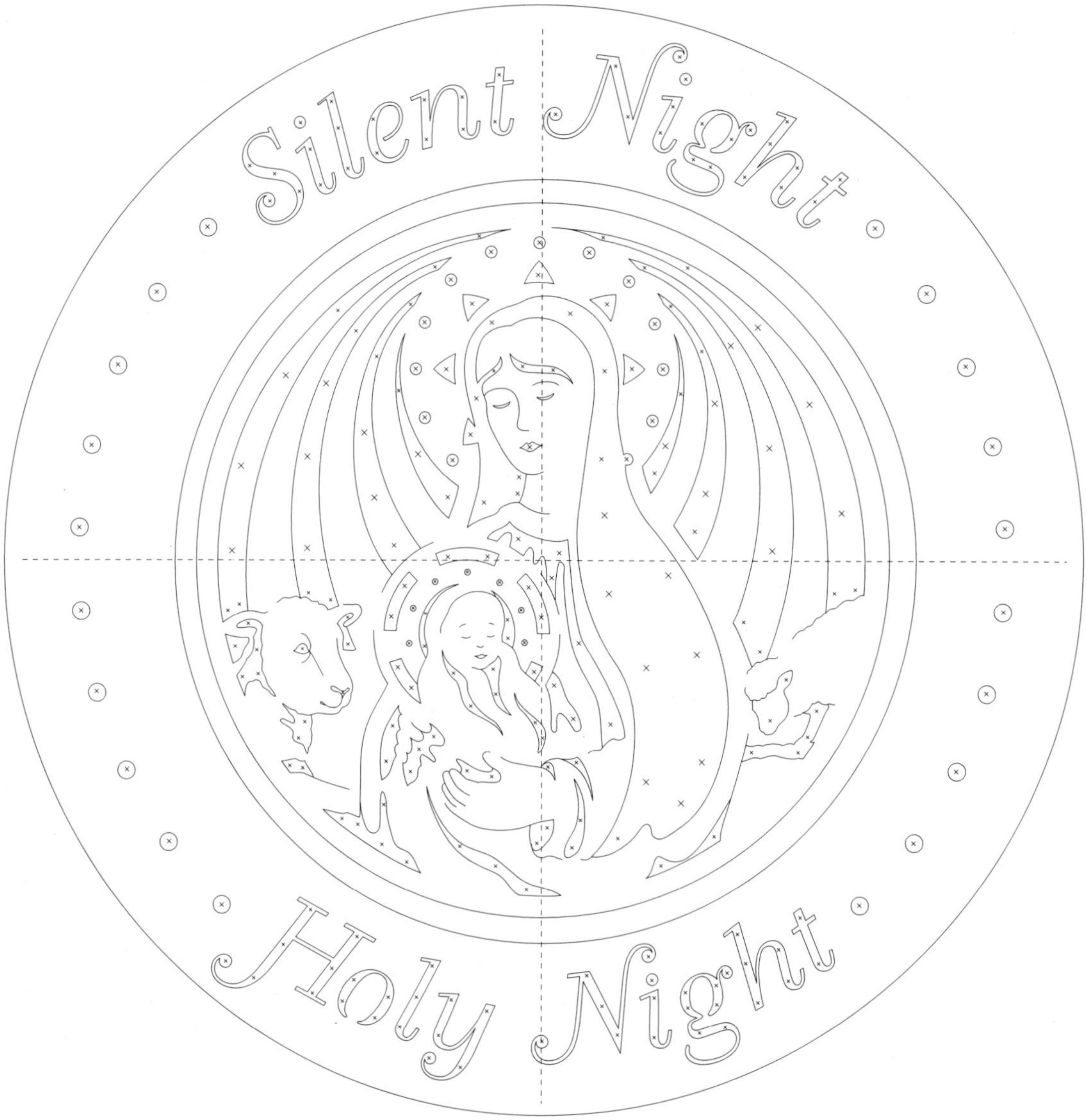

To decorate Silent Night, *cut an 8"-diameter circle from a piece of gold felt and use hot glue, epoxy, or white glue to permanently attach the felt to the back of the plate. Use a woodburner to burn the detail on the child's face and on the mother's eyes and eye brows. I found three sizes of gold beads that closely matched the drilled holes used throughout this design. The largest hole around the rim took a 5mm bead, the mother's halo used 3mm, and the child's was the smallest available. Use epoxy to glue the beads in place. Use a woodburner to accentuate the line work created by the scroll saw.*

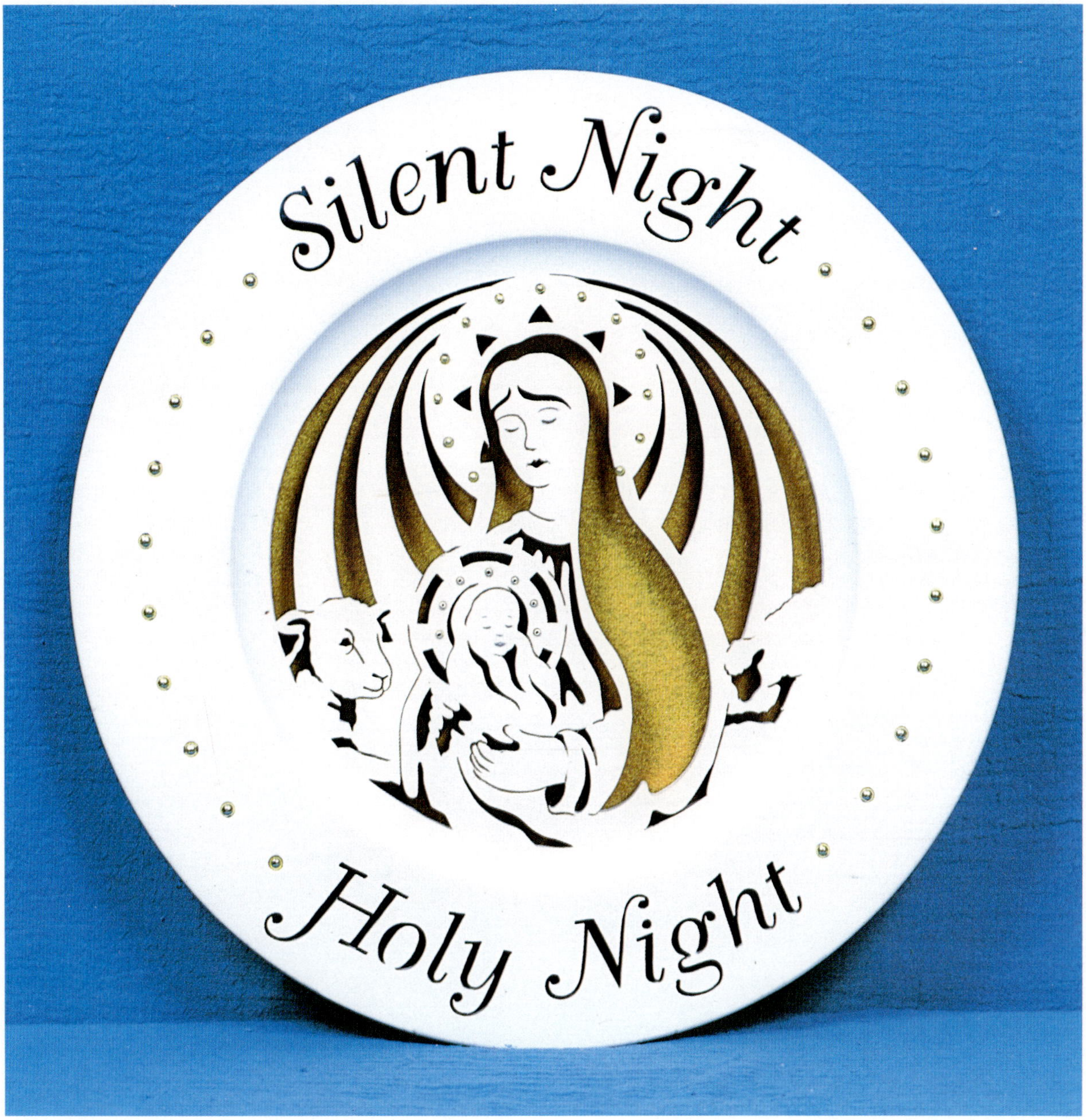
Silent Night
Holy Night

Southwestern Bird

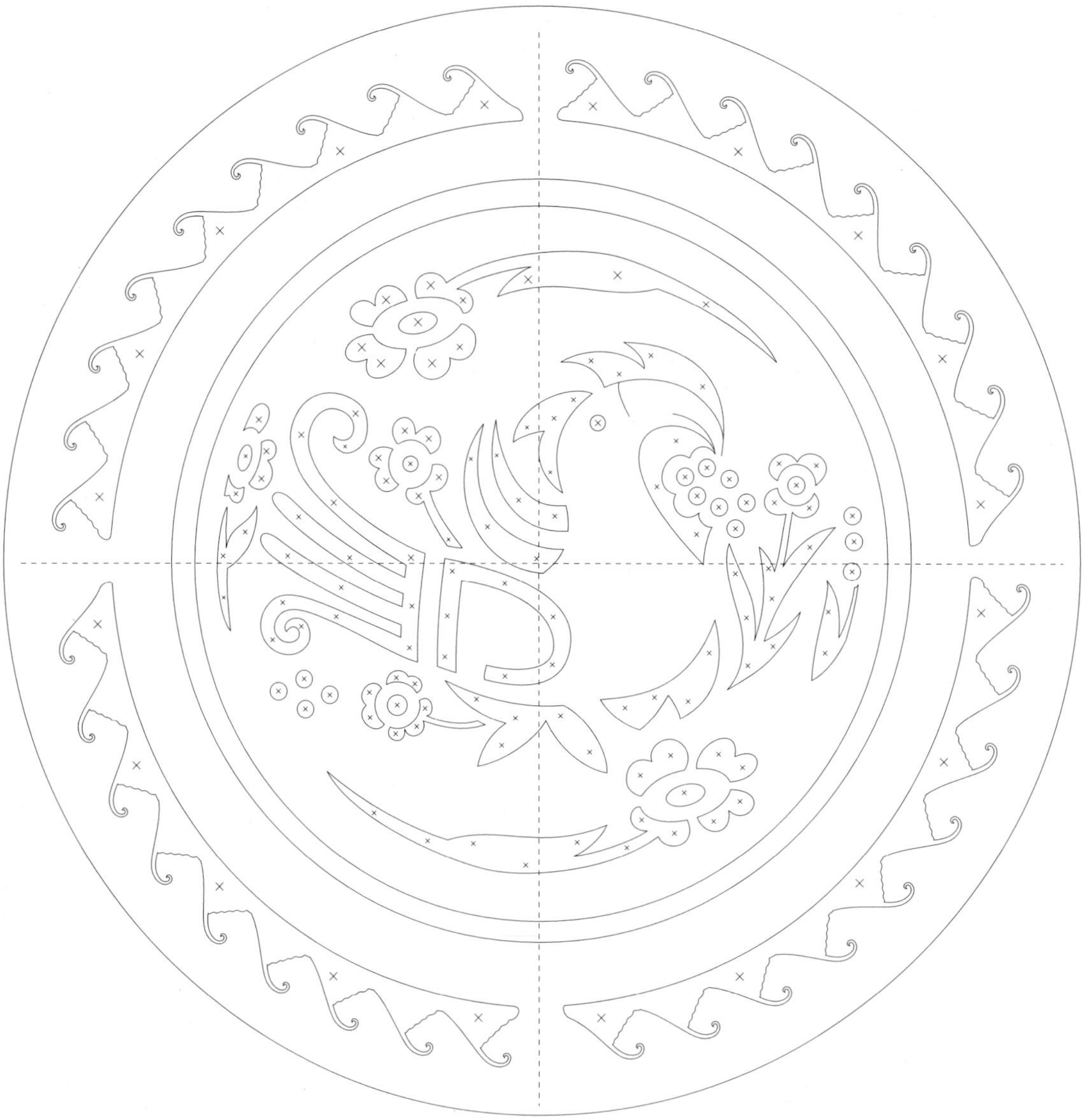

To decorate Southwestern Bird, *cut an 8"-diameter circle from a piece of turquoise paper. Use hot glue, epoxy, or white glue to permanently attach the paper to the back of the plate. You may also want to glue different colored beads or pom-poms in the drilled sections.*

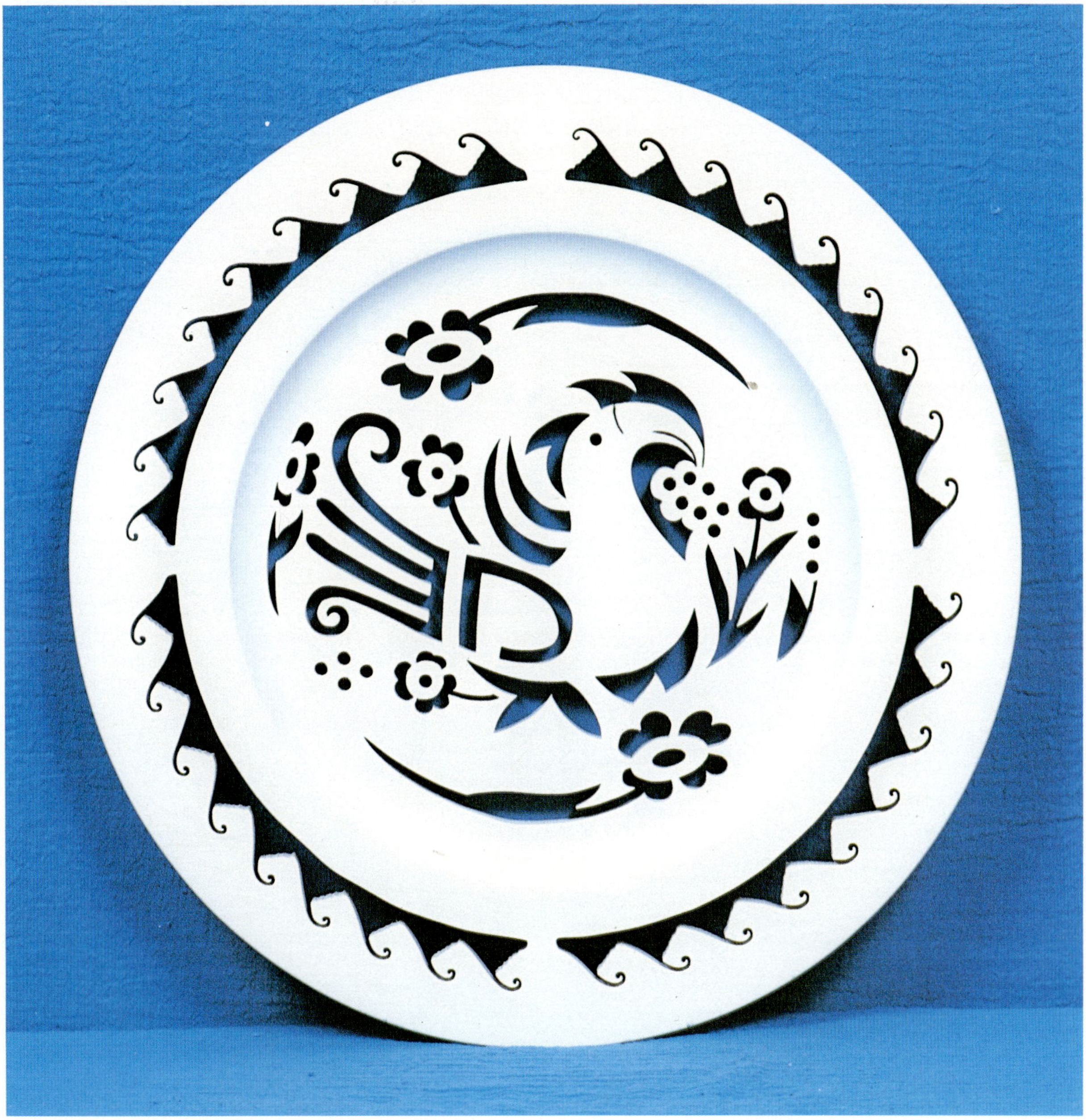

Stained-Glass Rose

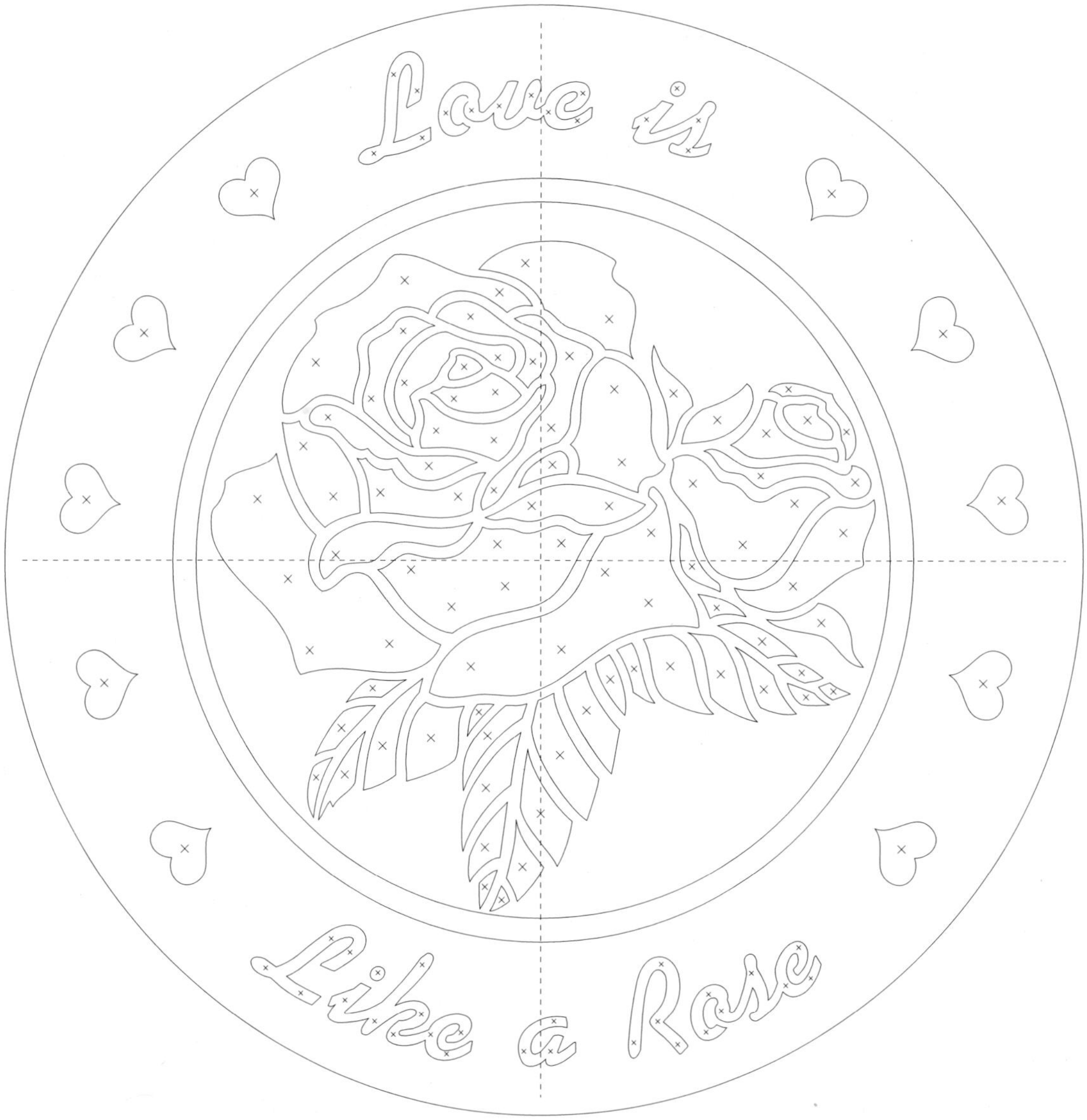

To decorate Stained-Glass Rose, *cut an 8"-diameter circle from a piece of plexiglass. Following the outlines on the scroll-saw pattern, use water-based glass paint to paint the rose on the plexiglass. When the paint dries, attach the plexiglass to the back of the plate with epoxy, hot glue, or screws. You may want to use this pattern for the center of the* Anniversary *plate.*

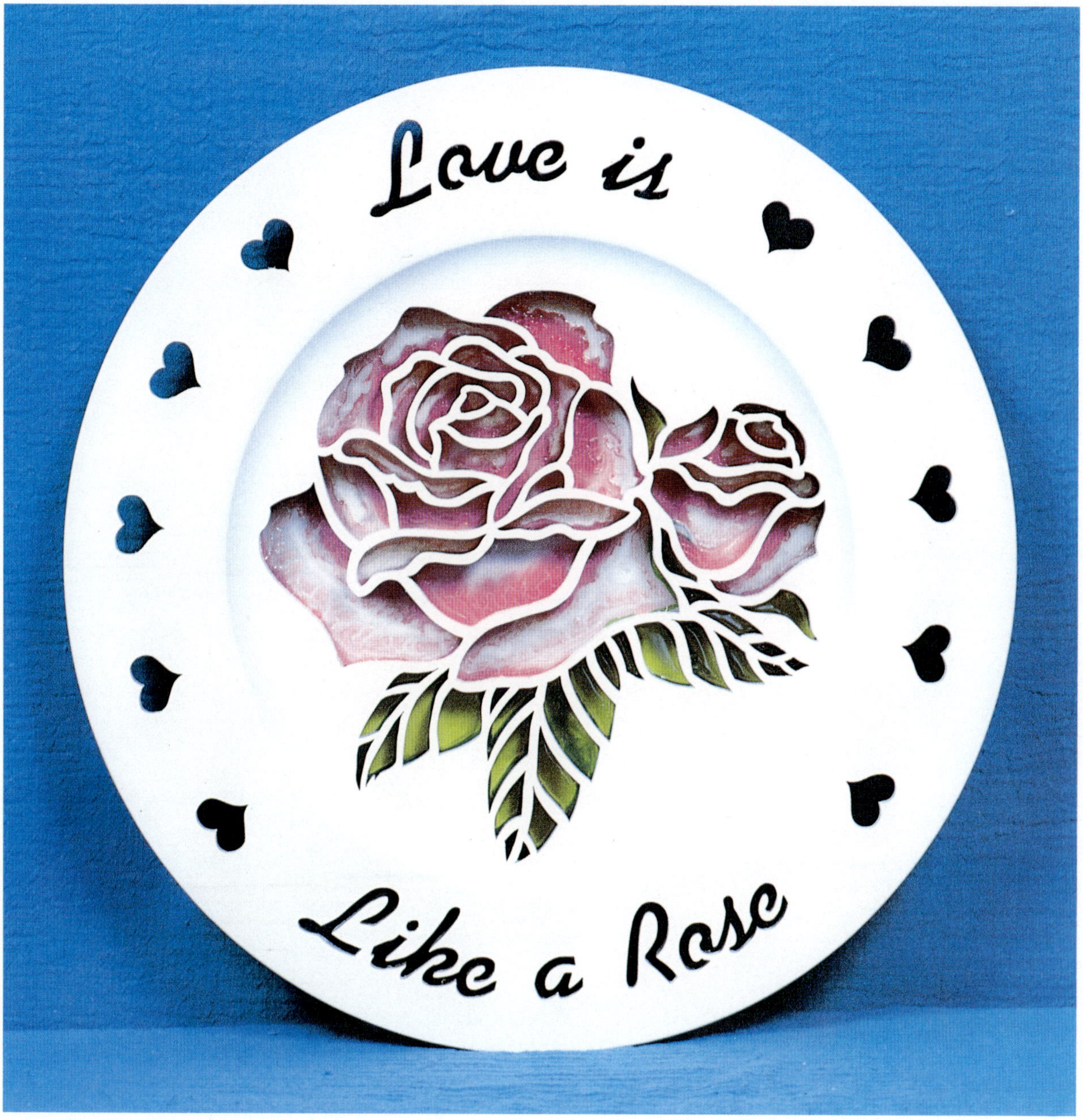
Love is
Like a Rose

Mom's Kitchen

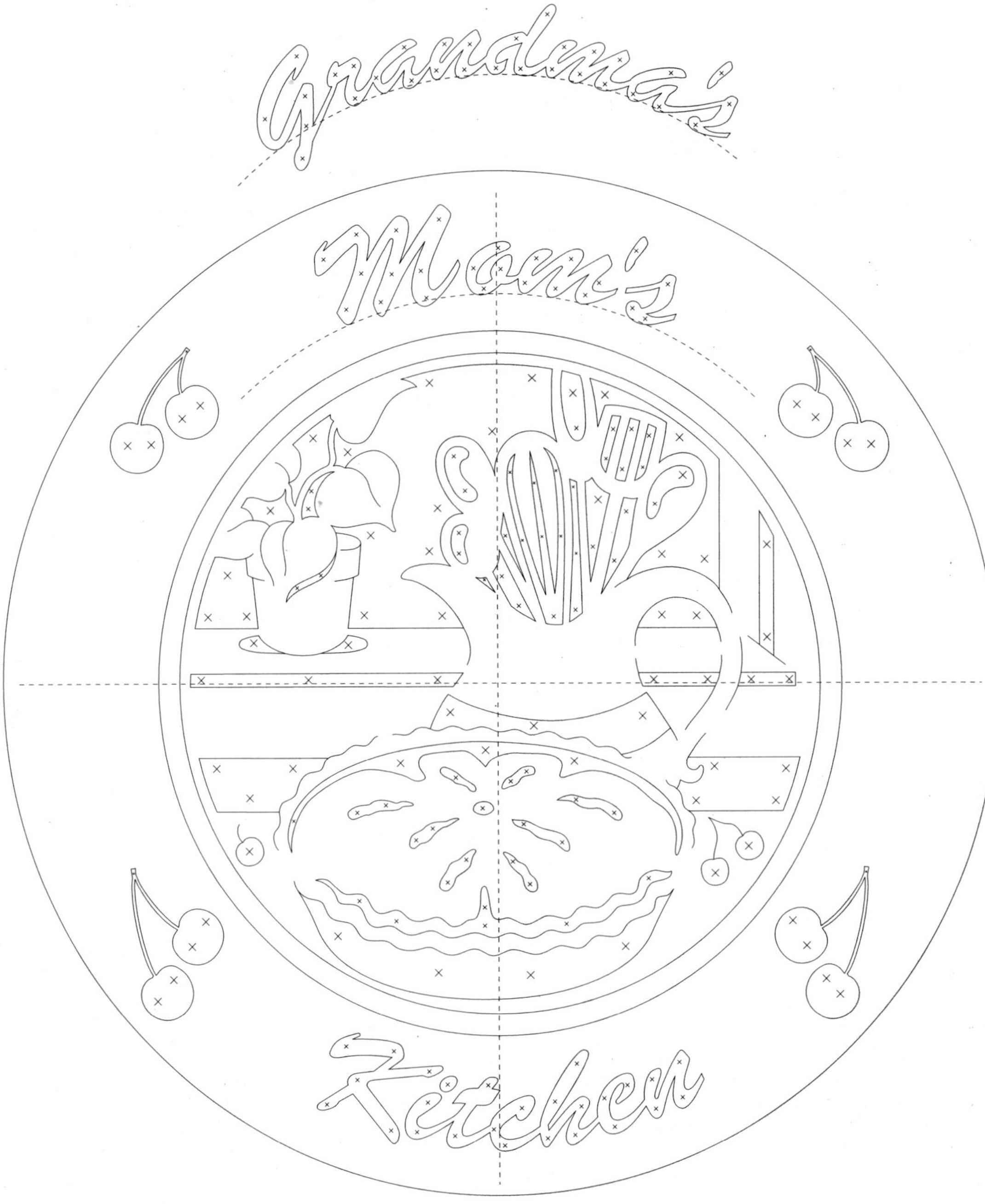

To decorate Mom's Kitchen, cut an 8"-diameter circle from red poster board. Use hot glue, epoxy, or white glue to permanently attach the backing to the plate. To accentuate the line work created by the scroll saw, use a woodburner. Use the additional type to change "Mom's Kitchen" to "Grandma's Kitchen." You can also add a wash of colors with oil color pencils. These pencils are semi-opaque, so the woodgrain can still be seen through the color. Use a light coat of clear acrylic to help preserve the color.

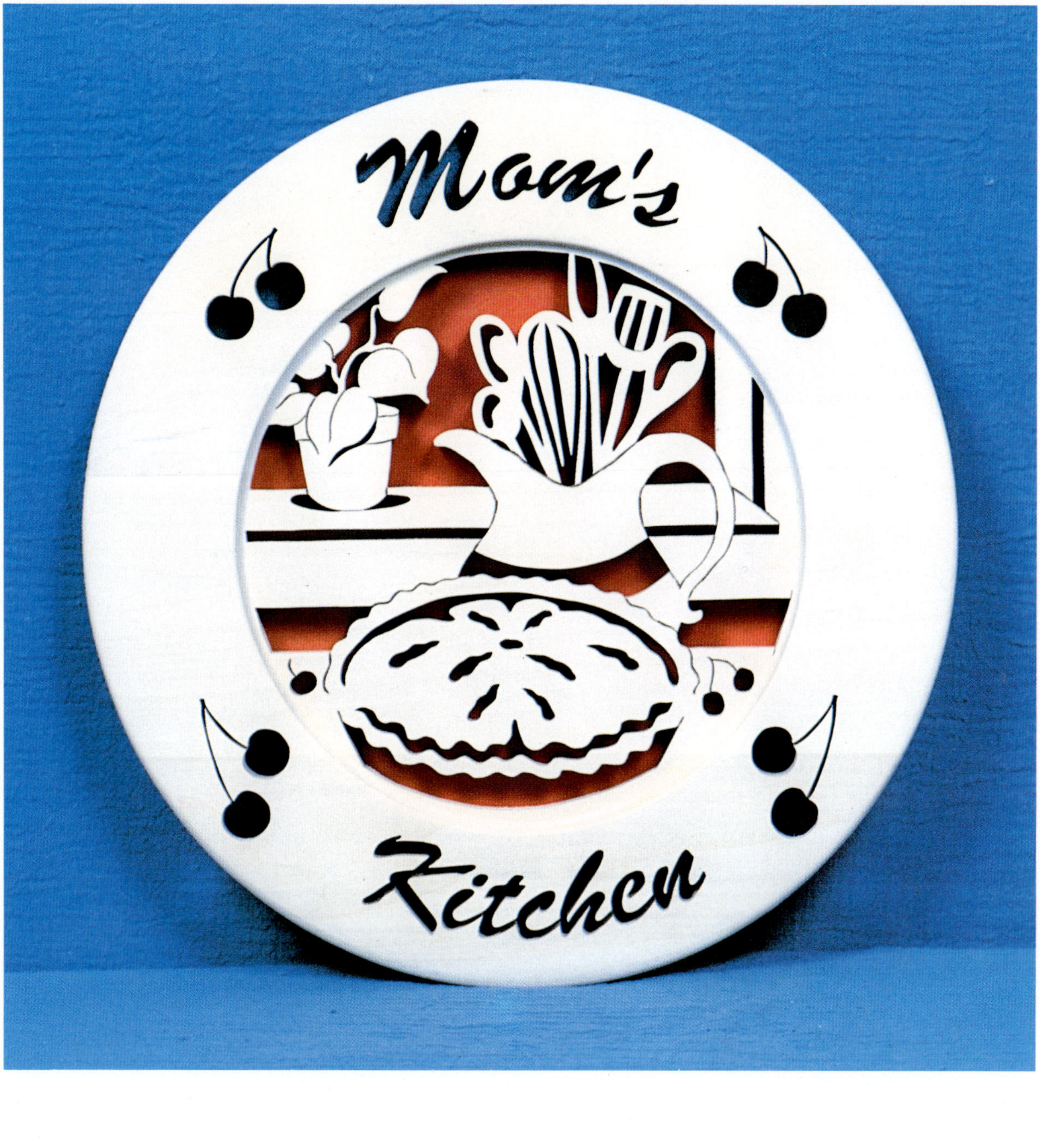
Mom's
Kitchen

God Loves All Creatures

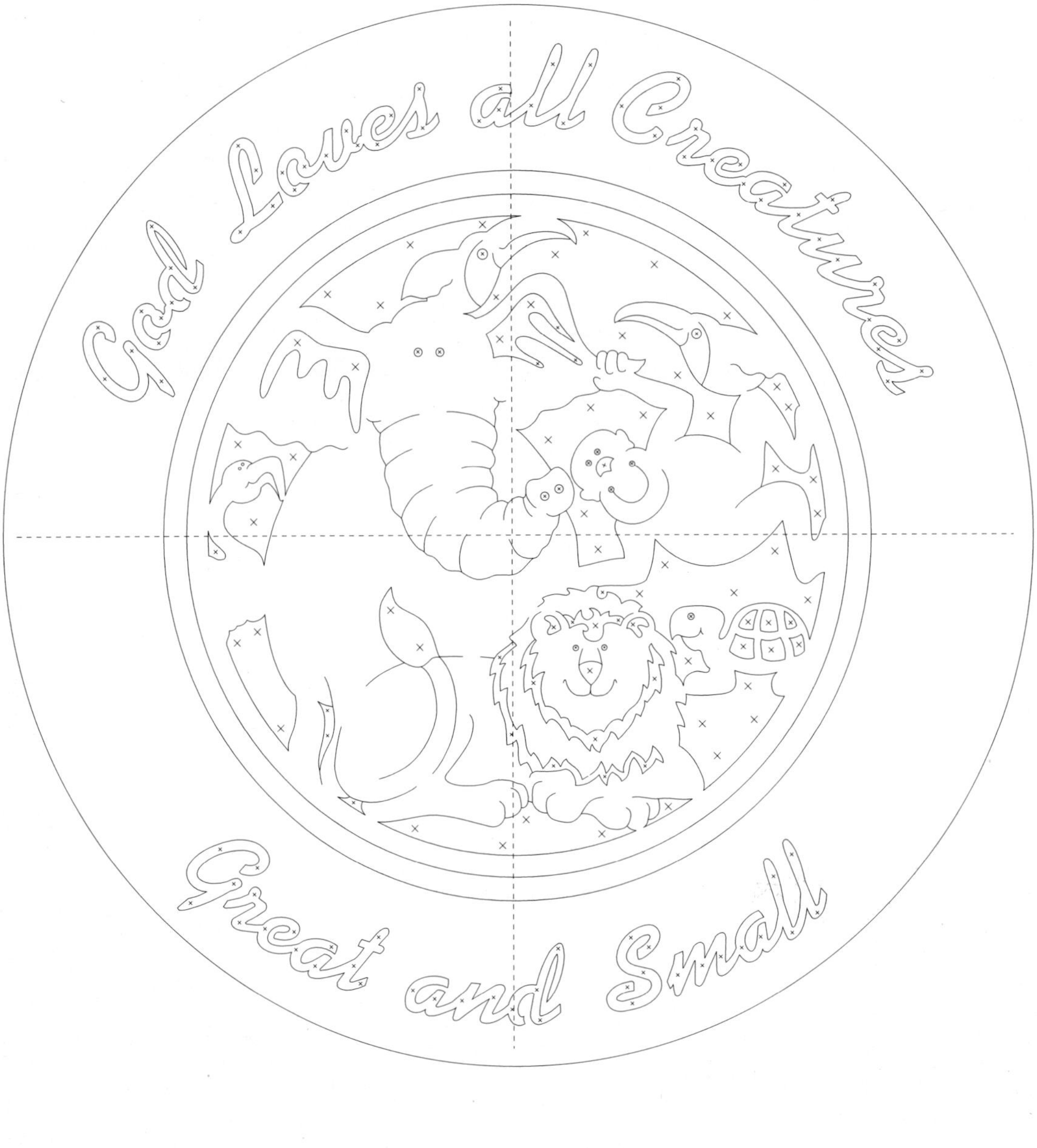

To decorate God Loves All Creatures, *use a woodburner to accentuate the line work created by the scroll saw. Also use the woodburner to add detail to the eyes if they are too small to drill. For this plate, we used a woodburner on the flamingo's and lion's eyes. You may also want to add a wash of colors to the animals with permanent markers. The markers are easy to control and are transparent, so the woodgrain will show through the color. If you plan to use markers, first separate the animals with a woodburner to keep the colors from bleeding on to the adjoining animal. Oil color pencils, a semi-opaque medium, will also allow the grain to show through. Finish the plate with a light coat of clear acrylic to help preserve the color.*

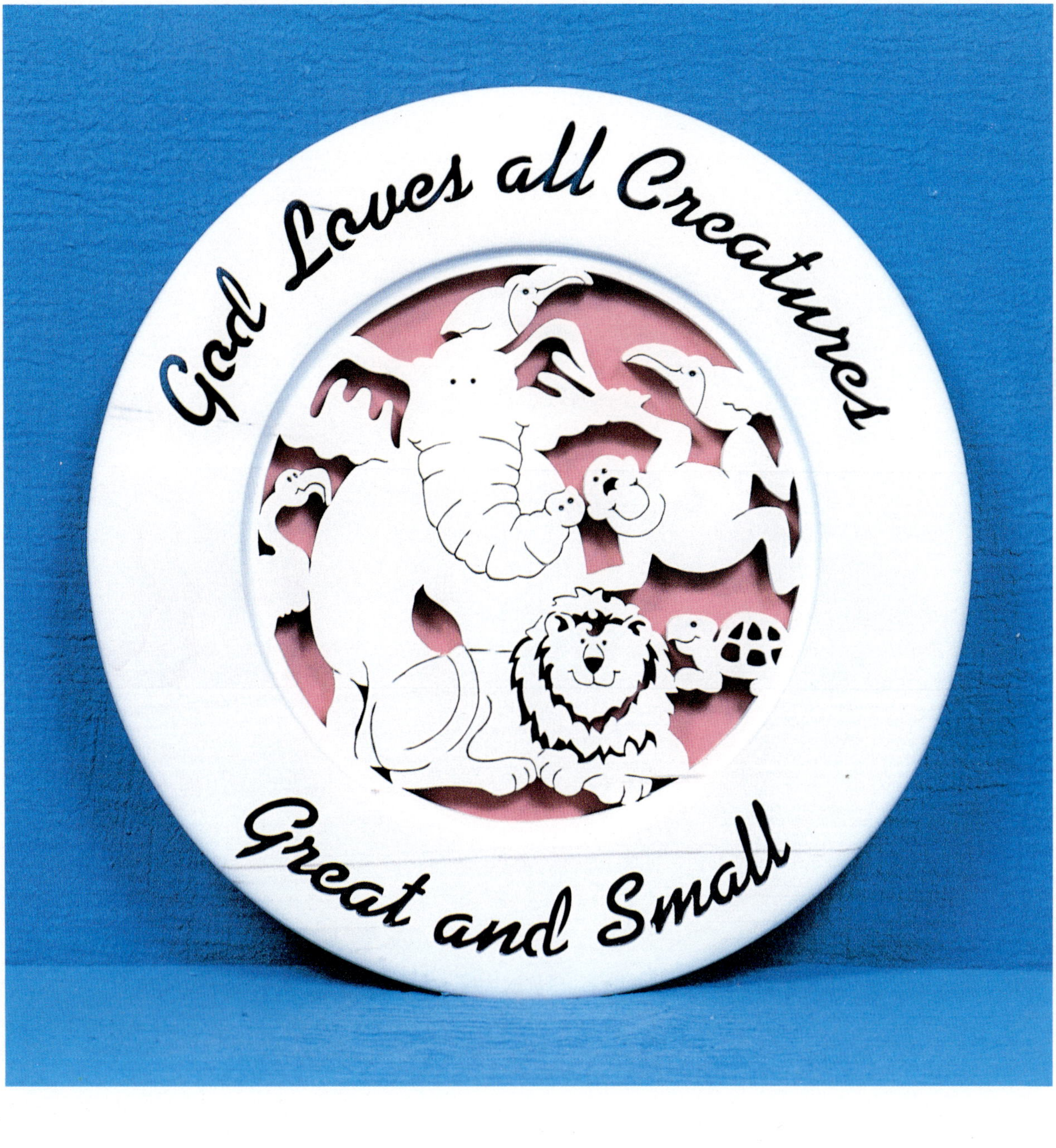
God Loves all Creatures
Great and Small

Anniversary

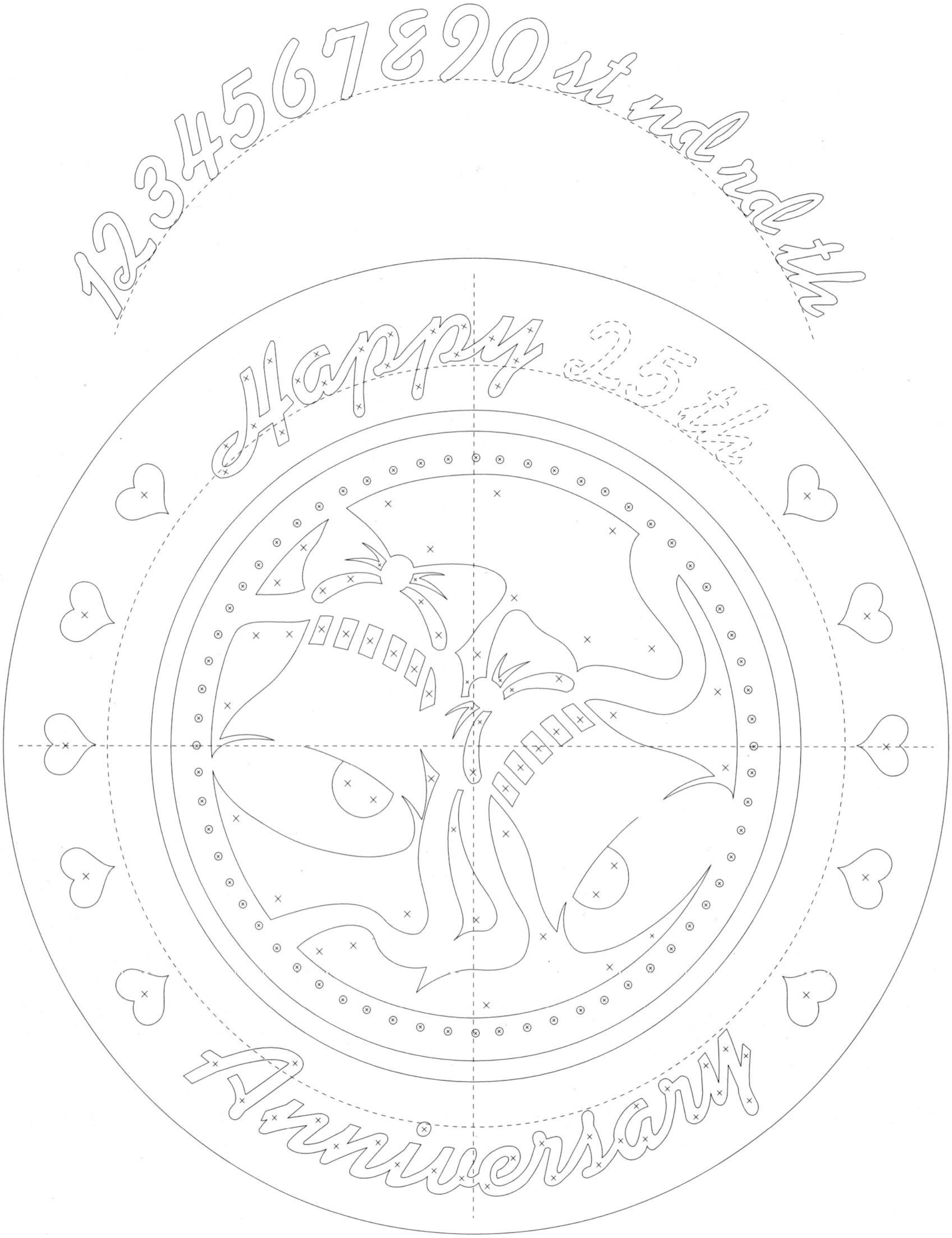

To decorate Anniversary, cut an 8"-diameter circle from a piece of gold fabric and use hot glue, epoxy, or white glue to permanently attach the fabric to the back of the plate. Lace white cord with gold metallic accents in and out of the drilled holes. You can also glue different color beads, small flowers, small bows, or pom-poms in the drilled sections, lace ribbon in and out of the bells, or stuff pom-poms in the hearts. Change the text by adding different numbers to the outer rim.

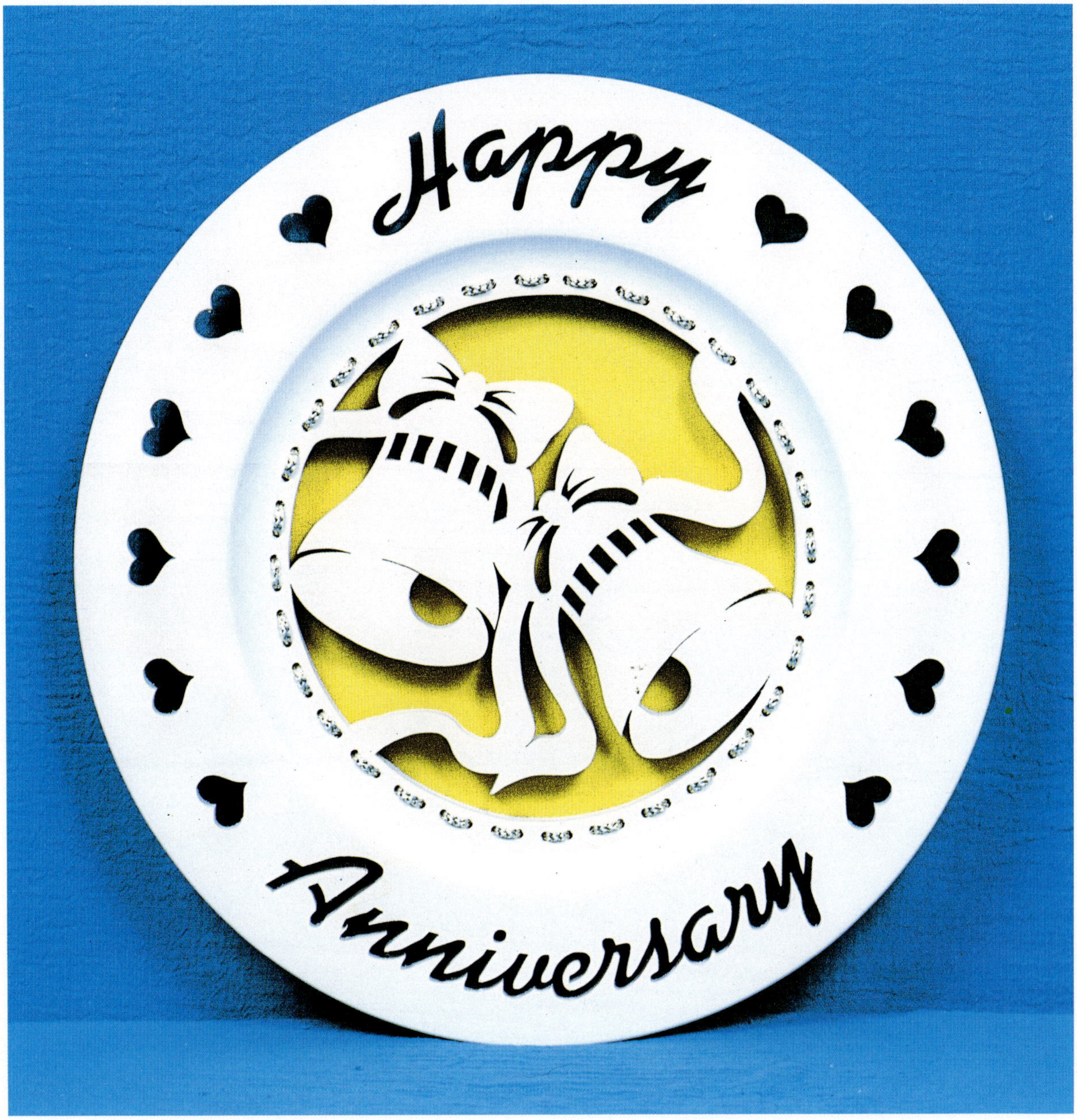
Happy
Anniversary

God Bless This House

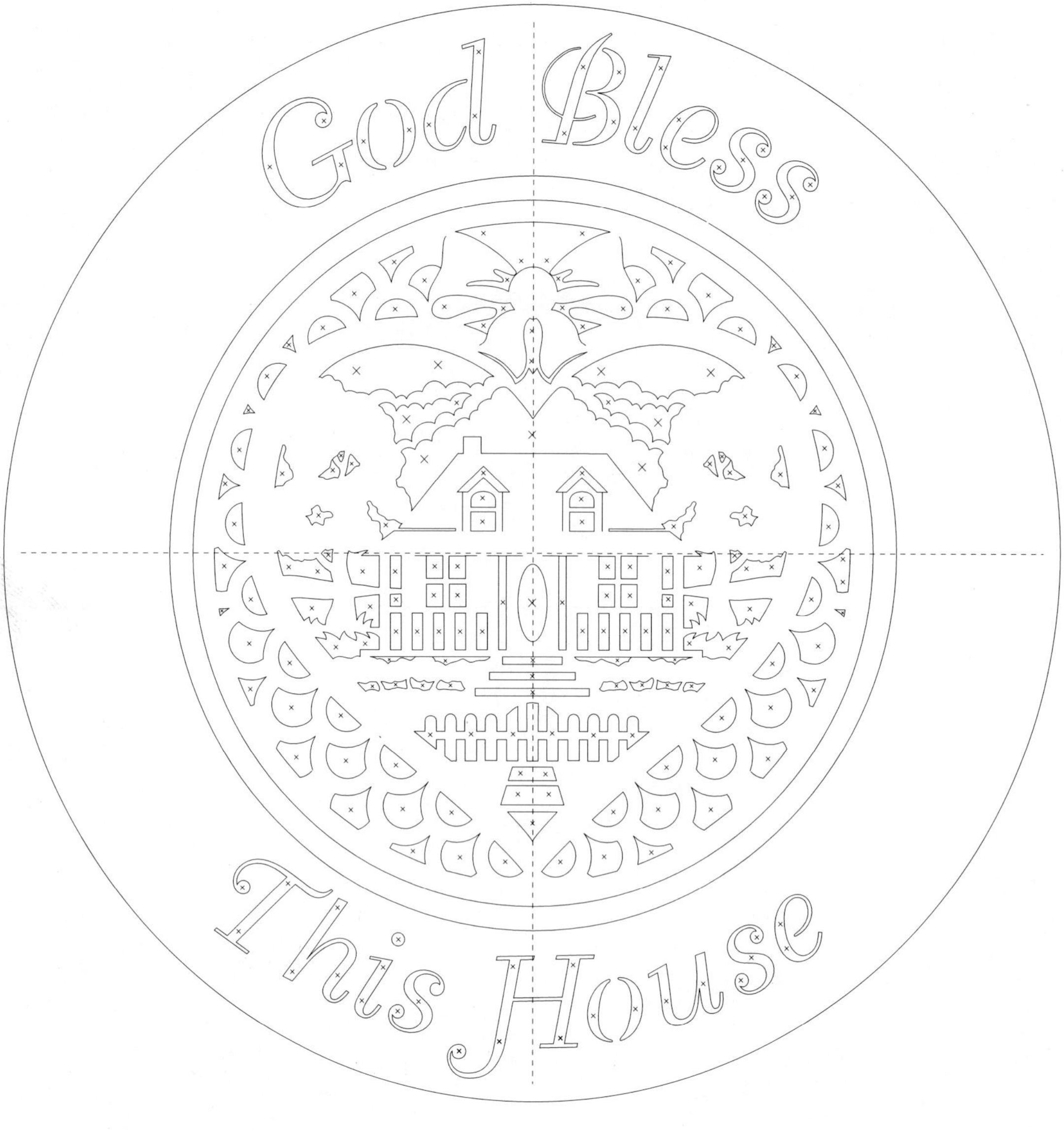

This plate has so many intricate cuts, I was afraid to decorate it. I did not want to detract from the plate by adding more to the design. I simply glued a light blue piece of poster board, 8" in diameter, to the back of the plate. You may want to add some small bows, beads, or pom-poms, perhaps the same color as the background, around the rim of the plate.

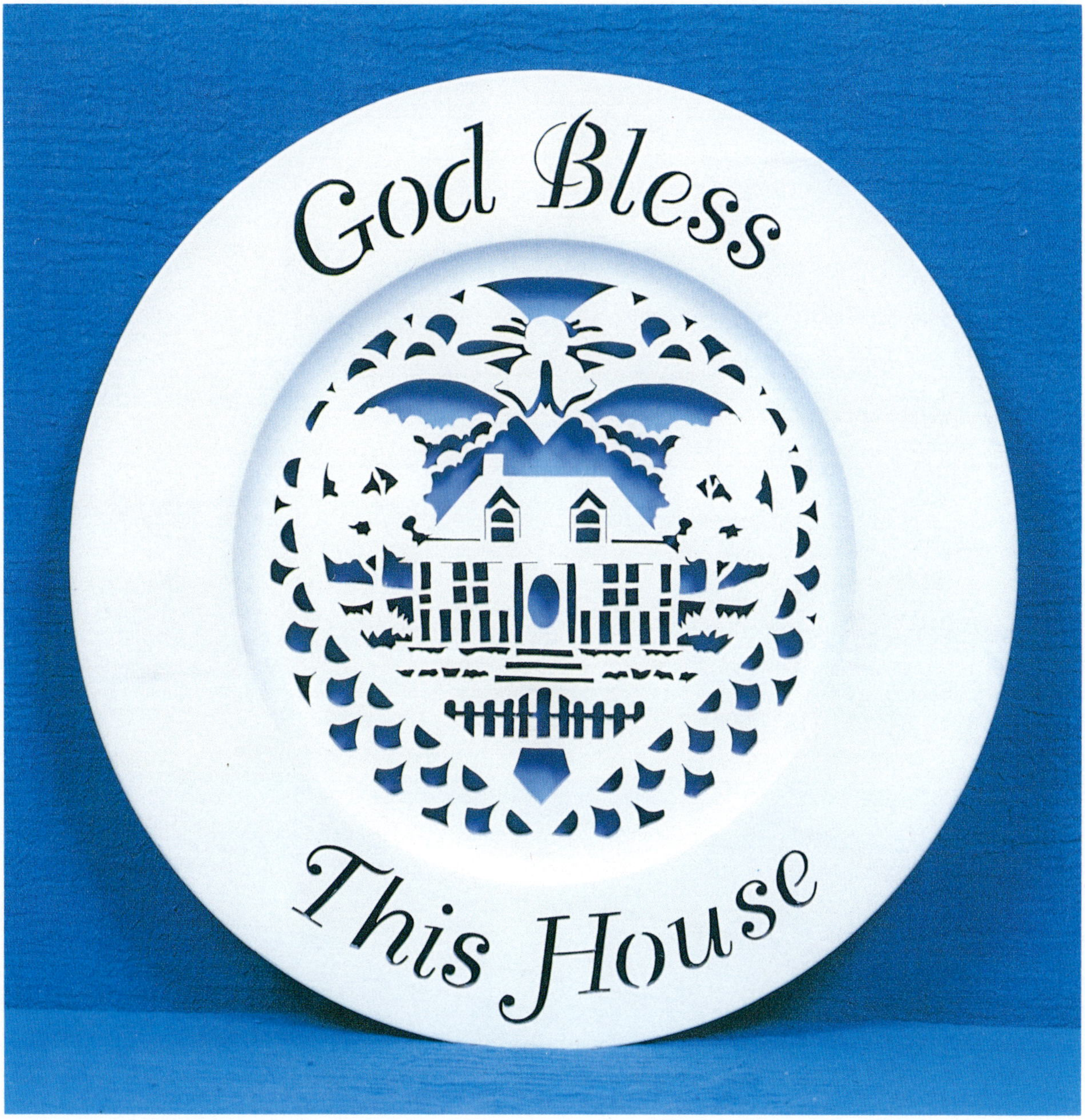
God Bless
This House

Buyers Guide

Plate Kits

The designs included in this book are available in a full size pattern plate kit. To purchase one of the plate kits, contact your local woodworking supply dealer, or your favorite woodworking mail order catalog. You may also order by phone, toll free. The pattern plate kits are $15.95 each. Blank plates are $14.95 each, plus shipping and handling.

Credit card orders only (MC and Visa)
(800) 316-9010
(409) 632-9663
Pattern Masters
PO Box 550
Lufkin, Texas 75902

Engraving Systems

Paragrave Corporation
1455 West Center
Orem, Utah 84057
(800) 624-7415

Wiping Gel Finish

For the dealer nearest you call
Bartley Wiping Gel
(800) 227-8539

Index

The Mott Miniature Furniture Workshop Manual
by Barbara and Elizabeth Mott
THE book for miniature furniture hobbyists. Jam-packed with techniques and patterns. Contains ready to use detailed patterns for 144 projects- from windsor chairs to rocking horses-all to scale. Information on miniature chair caning, wood bending, assembly instructions carving techniques. Over 100 ready to use miniature prints, photos and decals included.
Soft cover, 220 pages
ISBN# 1-56523-052-3 **$19.95 retail**

Mammals: An Artistic Approach
by Desiree Hajny
Your chance to learn from one of the world's top notch carvers. Features a helpful step-by-step photo session as Desiree carvers an otter. Learn the carving, texturing and painting techniques that have brought worldwide recognition of her work. Patterns, anatomy studies and reference photos are inside for deer, bears, otters and more. Color section PLUS a gallery section showing some of her outstanding pieces over the years. Heavily illustrated Softcover, 180 pages.
ISBN # 1-56523-036-1 **$19.95 retail**

Carving Wooden Critters
Includes power carving techniques by Diane Ernst
Diane Ernst's first pattern treasury.
A frequent award winner for her cute puppies, rabbits and other critters, Diane's patterns feature multiple views-top, side, front and back and also include wood burning details. A step by step photo session using power carving tools is also included. Buy this book and start carving your own character-filled critters.
ISBN # 1-56523-038-8 **$6.95 retail**

Woodcarving Books
by George Lehman
Learn new techniques as you carve these projects designed by professional artists and carver George Lehman. These best-selling books by a master carver are invaluable reference books, PLUS each book contains over 20 ready-to-use patterns.

Book One - Carving Realistic Game and Songbirds - Patterns and instructions
Enthusiastically received by carvers across the US and Canada. George pays particular attention to the needs of beginning carvers in this volume. 20 patterns, over 70 photos, sketches and reference drawing.
96 pages, spiral bound, 14 x 11 inches, includes index, resources
ISBN# 1-56523-004-3 **$19.95**

Book Two - Realism in Wood - 22 projects, detailed patterns and instructions
This volume features a selection of patterns for shorebirds and birds of prey in addition to all-new duck and songbird patterns. Special sections on adding detail, burning.
112 pages, spiral bound, 14 x 11 inches, includes index, resources
ISBN# 1-56523-005-1, **$19.95**

Book Three - Nature in Wood - patterns for carving 21 smaller birds and 8 wild animals
Focuses on songbirds and small game birds . Numerous tips and techniques throughout including instruction on necessary skills for creating downy feather details and realistic wings. Wonderful section on wild animal carvings with measured patterns.
128 pages, soft bound, 11 x 8.5 inches, includes index, resources
ISBN #1-56523-006-X **$16.95**

Book Four - Carving Wildlife in Wood- 20 Exciting Projects
Here is George's newest book for decorative woodcarvers with never-before-published patterns. Tremendously detailed, these patterns appeal to carvers at all skill levels. Patterns for birds of prey, ducks, wild turkey, shorebirds and more! Great addition to any carvers library - will be used again and again.
96 pages, spiral-bound, 14 x 11 inches, includes index, resources
ISBN #1-56523-007-8 **$19.95**

Carving Kids
with Ivan Whillock
Brand new title from the author of pictorial Relief Carving, and Carving the Head in Wood. Master carver Whillock now turns his talents to carving an engaging series of children's portraits at play - playing baseball, dressing up in Mommy's clothes - ten different projects. Carving techniques are illustrated step-by-step, PLUS complete patterns are included. Full color project gallery. Over 100 illustrations.
ISBN# 1-56523-045-0 **$12.95 retail**

Easy to Make Wooden Inlay Projects: Intarsia
Intarsia is a method of making picture mosaics in wood, using a combination of wood grains and colors. The techniques and step-by-step instructions in this book will have you completing your own beautiful pieces in short order. Written by acknowledged expert Judy Gale Roberts, who has her own studio and publishes the Intarsia Times newsletter, produces videos, gives seminars and writes articles on the Intarsia method. Each project is featured in full color and this well written, heavily illustrated features over 100 photographs and includes index and directory of suppliers 250 pages, soft cover, 8.5 x 11 inches
ISBN# 56523-023-X **$19.95 retail**

Scroll Saw Woodcrafting Magic! Complete Pattern and How-to Manual
Includes complete patterns drawn to scale. You will be amazed at how easy it is to make these beautiful projects when you follow Joanne's helpful tips and work from these clear, precise patterns. Never-before-published patterns for original and creative toys, jewelry, and gifts. Never used a scroll saw? The tutorials in this book will get you started quickly. Experienced scroll-sawyers will delight in these all-new, unique projects, perfect for craft sales and gift-giving. Written by Joanne Lockwood, owner of Three Bears Studio in California and the president of the Sacramento Area Woodworkers; she is frequently featured in national woodwork and craft magazines. 180 pages, soft cover, 8.5 x 11 inches
ISBN# 1-56523-024-8 **$14.95 retail**

More great scroll saw books by Judy Gale Roberts!
Fine Line Designs Scroll Saw Fretwork Patterns
Especially designed for the scroll saw enthusiast who wishes to excel, the 'fine line design' method helps you to control drift error found with thick line patterns. Each book features great designs, expert tips, and patterns on oversized (up to 11" x 17" !) sheets in a special "lay flat" spiral binding. Choose the original Design Book 1 with animal and fun designs, or Design Book Two featuring "Western- Southwestern" designs.

Scroll Saw Fretwork Pattern, Design Book One "The Original"	$14.95
Scroll Saw Fretwork Patterns, Design Book Two "Western-Southwestern"	$16.95
Scroll Saw Fretwork Patterns, Design Book Three " The Great Outdoors" Patterns for a variety of wildlife, hunting and fishing scenes.	$14.95
Scroll Saw Fretwork Patterns, Design Book Four "Sports". Patterns for almost every type of sport activity - baseball, football, basketball ... and more.	$14.95
Scroll Saw Fretwork Patterns, Design Book Five "Heartland- Farm & Country". Great country woodworking designs and scenes.	$14.95
Scroll Saw Fretwork Patterns, Design Book Six " Pets & People" Creative patterns for dog, cat and pet-lovers.	$14.95

To Order: If you can't find these at your favorite bookseller you may order direct from the publisher at the prices listed above plus $2.00 per book shipping.
Send check or money order to:

Fox Chapel Publishing
Box 7948D
Lancaster, Pennsylvania, 17604